Two components emerge from the beautiful testimonies in this book: encouragement from older ministers and opportunity to taste the ministerial life. These constitute the ecology of the calling congregations we so desperately need today. May these words of witness enrich the ecclesial soil around us and nurture the call to gospel work in the lives of men and women.

Dwight A. Moody
Founder and First President, Academy of Preachers

The mark of a good book is the way it gains purchase on the reader as he or she goes along and finally leaves its stamp on the reader, who has been happily changed by the encounter. This is what happened to me as I read *Call Stories*. Maybe we pastors and preachers give too little thought, as the years go on, to our sense of calling and how it continues to figure into our service year after year. The testimonies of the contributors to this book reawakened my own sense of having been called to a life of ministry and left me refreshed and happy about my own spiritual journey. Thanks to all of you for brightening my life!

John Killinger
Distinguished Professor, Author, and Theologian

Call Stories is a must read for active ministers, for persons who are trying to discern if God is calling them to ministry, and for lay people who want to understand better the call to ministry. What emerges from this book are the stories of more than 40 persons who have experienced the call to be a pastor. No two stories are the same. Encouraging persons, congregations that gave young people an opportunity to grow, seemingly ordinary events that became a part of the providential call—all of these became a part of God's initial call to ministry and the process in which God continues to shape pastors as they grow in their understanding of God's continuing call to be a pastor.

Chuck Bugg
Preaching Coach, The Center for Healthy Churches

Stories are often the best way to communicate faith experiences that cannot be explained in concrete, rational ways. Writers of the biblical narratives understood this well. Meaning and insight for our own experiences become clearer through the stories of others. Barry Howard has done a great service to the faith community by gathering stories of call among clergy. The book is useful to anyone—lay or clergy alike—looking for clarity in their own unfolding awareness of callings.

Michael Wilson
Director, Center for Congregational Resources, Samford University

Moses saw a burning bush in the desert. Paul saw a bright light on a road. Jesus was in a synagogue reading the Torah. Brother Harold was in a mountain laurel thicket. Jane was in a Georgia camp around the campfire. The stories go on and on. You know those moments, those places where you claim that something or someone is claiming you. The where or how does not really matter, and the what is sometimes less than clear. What *is* clear is that something inside and beyond one's self is calling you to be and/or to do something that is sometimes yet to be fully determined. The clammy hands, the fluttering stomach, the clarity of mind, the focus of spirit—all ways to describe those moments when you are "called" to be and to do. It helps us to read the stories of others. And this collection of "call stories" calls us first to carefully listen, but to be alert. Perhaps the voice of God will even be calling you as you read.

Linda McKinnish Bridges
Founding Faculty Member and Later President, Baptist Seminary of Richmond

Call Stories is a collection of autobiographical accounts from pastors who come from a Baptist heritage, including men, women, and a few multigenerational clergy families. Stories of calling to ministry reflect not only individual experiences of divine summons, personal struggle, and affirmation but also cultural and denominational change spurred by the civil rights and women's movements and the expansion of theological education. This volume would be an excellent resource in congregations for laity exploring ministry as a vocation and in seminaries and divinity schools.

Penny Long Marler
Professor of Religion Emerita, Samford University

CALL
STORIES

Hearing and responding to God's call

Barry Howard, Editor

© 2019

Published in the United States by Nurturing Faith Inc., Macon GA,
www.nurturingfaith.net.

Library of Congress Cataloging-in-Publication Data is available.

ISBN: 978-1-63528-071-5

Contents

Introduction: Interpreting the Call

The call to be a pastor is a mystical and mysterious summons to help others navigate their spiritual journey, even as you navigate the maze of local church ministry.

How does one hear, sense, or interpret such a calling?

When I was growing up, I heard several pastors and evangelists share their call experiences. Most, but not all, were stereotypical stories that went something like this: God called. I resisted. God called again. I rebelled. God called yet again. I ran. God called one more time. I relented. I didn't want to be a pastor or preacher, but God had other plans.

While these testimonies sound like they were uttered by a few of the more reluctant Old Testament prophets, the bottom line is that most of the call stories I heard during my childhood had little joy. Many of the ministers gave the impression that God had robbed them of the good life they could have had by conscripting them into ministry.

When I sensed my own call to ministry at the age of 16, I was intrigued and delighted to hear my pastor say that he enjoyed ministry, both the preparation and the preaching, the pastoral leadership and the pastoral care. I am grateful for several wonderful pastoral mentors who helped me discover the joy of ministry and to channel "the fire in my bones" into a passion for pastoral work.

I remember how difficult it was to describe my sense of calling to others, even my closest friends and family. I once heard Dr. Fred Craddock say in describing the quandary of God's call, "I've never heard God call one to ministry in a voice the whole family can hear."

However one hears, senses, interprets, or understands this divine directive, a call to ministry should never be taken lightly. Pastoral ministry requires faithfulness, imagination, and determination. It is one of the only vocations where you are privileged to walk alongside people through every stage of life from birth to death. As churches, institutions, and communities experience a great paradigm shift, and as culture contends with diversity, paradox, and pluralism, the priestly and prophetic vocation of pastor may be more important than ever.

Four of Eugene Peterson's books about pastoral ministry have been extremely formative in helping me understand the uniqueness of a pastoral calling: *Five Smooth Stones of Pastoral Work, The Contemplative Pastor, Under the Unpredictable Plant,* and *The Pastor: A Memoir.* In a church world that looks to the pastor to be the CEO, a chaplain-on-demand, and an ecclesial entrepreneur, Peterson reminds ministers and churches that a pastor is more like a spiritual director, a "soul friend" who walks alongside others pointing out what God is doing in their life.

In a fast-paced world, where a competitive, consumerist culture has invaded the church, pastors are often expected to be an idealistic combination of captivating motivational speaker, savvy executive/administrator, and extraordinary counselor. But the call to be a pastor is unique. There is no other vocation like it.

For Peterson, the call to be a pastor is a call to spiritual discernment and caring within a unique local congregation and community. It is not a "one size fits all" occupation that functions uniformly in cookie-cutter churches. I believe that the "pastoral intelligence" you glean from ministering to your people becomes a primary tool of the Spirit that informs and inspires how you lead and preach to your congregation.

In *The Pastor: A Memoir*, Peterson summarizes his understanding of the biblical role of a pastor like this: "The pastor is not someone who 'gets things done' but rather the person placed in the community to pay attention and call attention to 'what is going on right now' between men and women, with one another and with God—this kingdom of God that is primarily local, relentlessly personal, and prayerful 'without ceasing.'"

In that same vein, veteran pastor Hardy Clemons reminds us that the church is to be "more family than corporation." Clemons reminds pastors and churches of the peculiarity of their mission: "Our goal is to minister; it is not to show a profit, amass a larger financial corpus, or grow bigger for our own security. The ultimate goals are to accept God's grace, share the good news, invite and equip disciples, and foster liberty and justice for all."

Each of us is responsible to God for fulfilling our calling. I confirmed my calling to be a pastor 43 years ago, and I am still learning, growing, and understanding more of what that means, even as my pastoral work takes on a different expression. Being a pastor is more than what I do; it is who I am called to be.

Every minister's call story is unique. Just as God reveals God's self in many ways, God also speaks and invites men and women to pastoral ministry in a variety of voices.

This volume is a collection of call stories from pastors representing a cross-section of Baptist life. Some, like me, were called at a very young age. Others were called to transition from successful careers in the marketplace. Some answered the call immediately, and others wrestled with the call before reaching a sense of clarity. These stories come from a menagerie of ministers representing diverse theological perspectives. The common denominators of this group are their Christian commitment, their Baptist heritage, and their unique call experience.

Behind almost every call story is a faithful yet imperfect congregation, supporting, affirming, and encouraging the future minister in his or her calling. I am grateful for these pastors who were willing to share their story, and for the congregations that helped them to flesh out their calling.

I love serving as a pastor. It is the only vocation I know of where you are privileged to share almost every circumstance of life with others. Despite the occasional heartaches and heartbreaks, my pastoral journey has overwhelmingly been filled with joy and a sense of mission.

Stories are inspiring. Who knows? Maybe one or more of the testimonials in this book will prompt some unsuspecting individuals to consider, claim, or clarify God's call and then serve with their best gifts.

Barry Howard

A Homespun Calling

Robert G. Baker

My dad and I left our family home outside of Georgetown, Ky., one Sunday morning in June of 1972. Driving on some of the curviest roads imaginable, we arrived about an hour later at a small, white-framed country church approximately five miles outside of Owenton. That little rural church was the Greenup Fork Baptist Church, located at a fork of Highway 845 between the tiny Owen County communities of Hesler and Monterey.

Normally on Sunday mornings neither my dad nor I would be going to Greenup Fork Baptist. Rather, on Sunday mornings we would be pulling out of the gravel driveway of our family home to make the short 15-minute drive to our home church—Midway Baptist in Midway, Ky.

My dad was a deacon and a Sunday School teacher, and I was a Midway Baptist "bed baby," having been raised in the church all of my growing-up years—from the time I was two weeks old (no kidding!) through my freshman year at Georgetown College. In truth, I was actually the "fill in" pianist for Midway Baptist at the time that my dad and I made that "anything but normal Sunday morning one-hour twisting and winding drive" to Greenup Fork Baptist.

Why were my dad and I traveling to Greenup Fork Baptist on that particular June Sunday morning in 1972? Why were we departing from our "normal" Sunday morning pattern?

The answer to these "why" questions is that some members of the congregation had asked me to come and preach at their Sunday morning worship service. To be totally transparent, that preaching invitation had actually been "delivered" by my dad who was a native of Owen County and who actually knew a few people at Greenup Fork Baptist.

That preaching invitation was, in and of itself, quite a surprise. As a 19-year-old college student who had just completed my freshman year, I was not accustomed to preaching. During my earlier teenage years, I had preached on two occasions at my home church in Midway. But I basically did that to please my pastor who had heard me give a five-to-eight-minute speech at an Elkhorn Baptist Associational Youth Speakers Tournament. Though I did not finish first in that speaking event, my pastor Byrd Ison (who thought that I should have won first place) came to the tournament and heard my short speech.

Shortly afterward, Brother Ison asked me to give my speech/sermonette during a Sunday evening worship service at Midway Baptist. I suppose I did okay because later he asked me to preach at two additional Sunday evening services.

1

Those few preaching/speaking occasions resulted in several Midway Baptist Church members occasionally coming up to me and saying things such as:

"Bobby, have you ever thought about becoming a preacher?"
"Bobby, I think you're going to be a preacher!"
"Bobby, don't you believe that God is calling you to preach?"

At the time I did not give those words and questions a second thought. Becoming a preacher was not on my vocational radar. There were various times during my teenage years when I thought I might possibly like to be a veterinarian. (I had grown up on a farm where we raised cattle, sheep, and hogs.) There was also a stretch as a teenager when I contemplated becoming a sales representative for some company or corporation. Becoming a high school teacher or college professor teaching math, English, and/or speech were also vocational goals that I contemplated during my teenage years. Sports broadcasting was yet another possible career that surfaced in my thoughts from time to time.

So, despite hearing those "Bobby, don't you think God is calling you to be a preacher?" comments from members of my church family, I did not at that point in my life perceive that God was calling me to enter the ministry and become a preacher.

Yet, my perception began to change on that June Sunday morning in 1972 when Dad and I navigated the curves, hills, and twisting turns that led us to Greenup Fork Baptist Church. Almost before we could get out of our car in the gravel parking lot, Dad and I were greeted by some of the nicest, friendliest people I had ever met. Even before we entered the church building, we had already met half of the people who came to church that morning. And we were warmly greeted soon after by the other half of the congregation—the people sitting in the pews of that small sanctuary waiting for the service to begin.

Mr. Marvin Miller, the 70-plus-year-old song leader (who was also the chairman of the deacons), gave me an order of service written on a white memo pad. We were to have an opening prayer, sing three hymns, take up the offering, and hear Mr. Miller's daughter Glenna sing a solo just before I preached.

"Brother Bob (that's what the people called me that day), we don't have a piano player, so we will just sing without a piano."

When I glanced at the hymns that had been selected, I realized I could play them in a halfway decent manner, so I volunteered to play the piano for the congregational singing. I preached the sermon (which lasted about 15 minutes), played the piano during the invitational hymn, thanked the folks for their hospitality, and then Mr. Miller gave the benediction.

Dad and I spent a few minutes outside on the front steps of the church talking to most all of the people who had come to worship. It didn't take all that long because there were only about 25-30 people in attendance that day (which was a big crowd for that rural congregation). Dad and I were heading to our car to drive back home when Mr. Miller flagged us down and asked if I could come back that night and preach at the evening service.

I was taken somewhat aback, but told Dad that I did have one other sermon I could preach, so I agreed to go back that evening.

On the drive back home, Dad and I talked about the service and shared with each other how nice and friendly all the people had been. Dad told me that I had "done well" preaching my sermon. (But I knew that my parents would tell me I did a good job of preaching even if I had really not done that well at all!) Still, Dad seemed genuinely sincere in sharing with me that the worship service had gone well.

Following Sunday dinner back home with my family, I read over the only other sermon I had in my two-sermon repertoire. I rested a bit, called my girlfriend Deborah (who one year later would become my wife), read the sports pages of the *Lexington Herald* newspaper, and listened to part of a Cincinnati Reds baseball game on the radio.

Late that afternoon Dad and I made the hour-long return drive to Greenup Fork Baptist. Mr. Miller once again led the singing (which were hymns I had selected because they were the ones I could play on the piano). I preached my only other sermon. One of the men in the congregation pronounced the benediction, and everyone gathered on the front lawn of the church to visit a while before going back to their homes.

Sometime during this "after church" gathering, Mr. Miller asked my dad and me if we could come back into the sanctuary. When we stepped back inside, we were joined by three other men who, along with Mr. Miller, were the four deacons of the church.

"Brother Bob, our deacons have just met, and we think God is calling you to be our pastor. Would you consider becoming our preacher here at Greenup Fork?"

I probably looked as dumbfounded as I felt. I was not planning to be a minister. I had just preached the only two sermons I had. I still had three years of college to finish. I had never even had a religion course. I wasn't even licensed to preach, much less ordained. I did not know the first thing about being a pastor.

Yet, there was something about the manner in which those four deacons asked me to consider being their pastor . . . something about the sincerity and the genuineness they conveyed . . . something about the hard-to-describe feelings I had in the midst of my dumbfoundedness and surprise . . . something that prevented me from saying, "Thank you, but there is no way I can or even should do this" . . . something that led me to say to those four deacons at the conclusion of what had been an anything-but-normal Sunday in June of 1972: "Let me think and pray about this for a week or so."

And those four deacons answered in what I can only describe as a hopeful, heartfelt way: "That's fine. We'll be praying for you as you consider what the Lord is calling you to do."

On the drive back home that evening, Dad and I talked about the surprising turn of events the day had brought. We discussed what God was calling me to do with my life. Our conversation continued with my mother when we arrived home. My parents never pressured me in any way as to what I should decide to do, but I knew they would support me and love me regardless of the decision I made.

The next week I talked with Brother Ison, my pastor. I had long conversations with Deborah, who up until that time had not considered that her "boyfriend and soon-to-be-fiancé and within-a-year-to-be-husband" might become a Baptist minister and that she might become a Baptist minister's wife. I had ongoing conversations with Mom and Dad. I found myself reflecting on those "Don't you think God might be calling you to be a preacher?" comments I had heard from members of my Midway Baptist Church family during my adolescent years.

Throughout that week I longed to hear God's voice. I so much hoped that God would just tell me what I was "supposed" to do—what the Lord desired for me to do. I would have given anything for an audible voice from heaven declaring that I was being called to preach.

As the week progressed, I came to realize that God had been and was continuing to speak to me. It was not in a loud audible voice, not in a dream, not through some dramatic or sudden "Damascus Road" experience. Rather, God had been "calling me" and "speaking" to me throughout my life: through loving Christian parents; through a home church that saw something in me that I, at the time, did not see in myself; through a pastor who encouraged me and who gave me my first preaching opportunities; through Deborah who supported me and loved me unconditionally; and through the people of the Greenup Fork Baptist Church who, on what proved to be an anything-but-normal Sunday back in June of 1972, not only invited a 19-year-old teenager to preach at their church, but also felt led of God to ask that 19-year-old to become their pastor.

I said yes to Greenup Fork's invitation. I was the church's pastor for the three remaining years of my college career. The congregation "put up" with my preaching and helped to make me a better preacher. They "taught me" much about being a pastor by going with me on visits to sick and homebound church members and to prospective church members. They helped me plan and conduct Vacation Bible School, which ministered to many children throughout the community. They assisted me in preparing for revival meetings. They invited Deborah and me to their homes for some of the most delicious home-cooked country meals imaginable.

When Deborah and I were married in June of 1973, the people of Greenup Fork came to our wedding held in Deborah's home church. When I was ordained by Midway Baptist in February of 1974, my church family from Greenup Fork came to my ordination service (traveling for more than an hour on snow-covered, slick, curvy roads). Through the love and encouragement Deborah and I received from our Greenup Fork congregation, we experienced invaluable "on the job" training regarding what it means to be a pastor and a pastor's wife.

During my three-year pastorate at Greenup Fork, my call to ministry was "solidified" by another person whom God placed in my life. At the beginning of my sophomore year at Georgetown College (about 2 ½ months after I began my pastorate at Greenup Fork), I enrolled in an "Introduction to the Old Testament" course taught by Dr. Joe Lewis. His intriguing and inspiring lectures and presentations introduced me to the historical-critical study of the Bible that enabled me to have a better understanding of and a greater appreciation for Holy Scripture.

Dr. Lewis taught me not only through his classroom lectures, but also through the life lessons he lived out as a Christian gentleman. He would often teach Bible studies and preach in local churches. He had this incredible knack for being able to make the Bible come alive, both for religion majors in the college classroom and for laity in the pew. His preaching/teaching gifts, coupled with his affable Christian lifestyle, resulted in Dr. Lewis becoming my role model and mentor.

My wife also was a student in Dr. Lewis' Old Testament class. What she gained from Dr. Lewis' teaching enabled her to become a most effective youth, college, and young adult Sunday School teacher in the churches where we have served. Our profound admiration for Dr. Lewis resulted in Deborah and myself asking Dr. Lewis to officiate at our wedding.

In addition to "marrying" Deborah and me, Dr. Lewis preached the sermon at my ordination, encouraged me to travel with him on a group tour of the Holy Land, recommended me for a scholarship at Southern Seminary (which I received), encouraged me to pursue a Ph.D. so that I would be better prepared to be a pastor and an adjunct professor, sent letters of recommendation on my behalf to the pulpit committees of the churches I have pastored, and served as the external reader of my doctoral dissertation.

Throughout my 46 years in pastoral ministry Dr. Lewis has continued to encourage me to "keep on keeping on" in attempting to live out my calling as a minister of the gospel—a calling I began to take seriously on that anything-but-normal Sunday evening back in June of 1972 when the deacons of the Greenup Fork Baptist Church in Owen County, Ky., asked me if I would consider becoming their pastor.

I am so glad they asked. I am so glad I felt "led" to accept. And I am so grateful for people like my parents, my pastor Byrd Ison, my professor/mentor Dr. Joe Lewis, and for the people of Midway Baptist and Greenup Fork. God "spoke" to me through these good and gracious Christians. They were instrumental in helping me recognize my "call" to pastoral ministry. Their influence continues to encourage me as I strive to "live out" God's ongoing call for my life.

Robert Baker retired in early 2019 as the senior pastor of Calvary Baptist Church in Lexington, Ky., where he served for 27 years.

Finding My Way Home

Mary Alice Birdwhistell

In her memoir *Traveling Mercies,* Anne Lamott tells a story about a little girl who was walking around town one day when she lost her way home. She ran up and down the streets, but the little girl didn't see anything that looked familiar. She became scared and unsure of what to do or where to go until a policeman saw her and stopped to help. They drove around town together in his police car until, suddenly, the little girl saw a familiar landmark: her church. Immediately she said to him, "You can let me out now. This is my church, and I know I can always find my way home from here."

Throughout my life there have been landmarks that have helped me find my way to my calling. The first would be Sand Spring Baptist Church in Lawrenceburg, Ky. My dad grew up at Sand Spring, and he and my mom met there. She sang in the church choir and directed the children's Christmas musical each year, and he was the Sunday School director and a deacon. I still remember eating Hershey's Kisses on Communion Sundays on the back pew with my grandmother and watching Bible stories come to life in Ms. Donna and Ms. Mary Jane's Sunday School class each week. I also remember starting a Christian band with my best friend and debuting our first song during the opening celebration of Vacation Bible School.

I first began to sense God calling me to ministry as a sixth grader at summer camp. Looking back, I have always asked myself if this was an overly emotionalized altar-call experience, and it probably was. However, I have never doubted that this is when I first began to hear a voice calling me to ministry—something I had never considered before. All I know is that something sparked to life within me that day at camp, and it has never gone away.

I am grateful that the good people at Sand Spring affirmed this calling in me in all the ways they knew how. My youth minister often asked me to teach Bible studies and to be a leader in our youth group, and my pastor even invited me to share testimonies in church on several occasions. I began to wonder if there was some kind of imaginary age when it suddenly wouldn't be okay for me to do things like this anymore, because all of the leaders, preachers, pray-ers, and even offering-takers I saw in the church were men. I remember asking why women couldn't be pastors, but I was taught that women weren't supposed to teach or have authority over men. "Besides," I was told, "we were simply too emotional to be pastors, and we couldn't handle all the funerals, hospital visits, and pastoral counseling" and "that's not what God created women to do." So, I soon dismissed the idea altogether.

About that time our children's director asked me to be her intern during the summers. She taught me so much, not only about ministry with children, but also about ministry within the church. Looking back, she was beautifully modeling for me what it looked like to be a pastor; she just wouldn't have called herself one. Although my home church would likely not ordain me today, the people there taught me to know and follow Jesus, and they equipped me for ministry in every way they knew how. So much of who I am today, I owe to them.

Another important landmark in my journey would be Georgetown College in Kentucky. At Georgetown I got my feet wet in a diversity of ministry experiences. I taught campus Bible studies, led spring break mission trips, worked on staff at summer church camps, and served as chaplain of my sorority. With each experience I continued to sense God calling me to ministry. Ironically, the dean of the chapel at Georgetown, Dwight Moody, encouraged me to preach from the very first time he heard me speak at a campus ministry event, but whenever he would mention it to me, I would always laugh at him and say, "Dr. Moody, women can't do that." He would just smile at me and shake his head, but he never gave up on me.

I remember the first time I heard a woman preach during chapel, and I had no idea what to do with her. I thought she was disobeying God, because God didn't call women to preach! It wasn't until I took a class called "Women in the Christian Tradition" during my junior year at Georgetown that I learned this topic wasn't as black and white as I was led to believe growing up. Through continued study and prayer, I began to think that it could be possible, and maybe even biblical, for God to call women to be pastors, but I couldn't imagine myself ever doing that. I didn't know of one Baptist church that would ever call a woman to be pastor, and I had no model for what this even looked like. I questioned whether friends or family would ever accept such a calling, especially one that I couldn't even understand myself. I continued to put pastoral ministry on the back burner, trying to convince myself that I must be better suited for another type of ministry.

About the same time one of our campus ministers, who was the pastor of a small Methodist church in the county, nonchalantly asked me on campus one day if I would preach for him on a Sunday. I was floored. I asked him if he meant to ask me, a woman, to preach in the pulpit on a Sunday morning. He stared back at me in disbelief, shocked that I had never done this before. I remember praying and asking if I could be disobeying God by accepting the invitation to preach, but I felt a sense of peace and even curiosity about it. A few days later I accepted the invitation.

I still remember seeing the sun rise as I drove out to the beautiful, old, white church in the country, early that Sunday morning. As I stepped into the pulpit that day, I immediately knew I had discovered something that made me come alive in a way I had never experienced before. It was both exhilarating and absolutely terrifying—all at the same time.

Near the end of my time in college Dwight Moody took me with a group of students to attend a Baptist gathering in Atlanta, Ga., where I heard Julie Pennington-Russell preach. I was absolutely mesmerized by her presence in the pulpit that day. Her sermon wove stories together in such a creative way, and she spoke with a passion and authenticity I hadn't encountered before from the pulpit. I didn't know sermons could even sound like that. I looked up at Dr. Moody and said, "Maybe I could do something like that one day, too." With a twinkle in his eye, he encouraged me to meet Julie, so I marched myself up to the front of the large convention center and stood in line to meet her. Little did either of us know how God would weave our stories together in the days and years to come.

About a year later I found myself at another landmark along my journey as a first-year student at Truett Seminary in Waco, Texas. I never thought I would move to Texas; in fact, I visited Truett to rule it out and mark it off my list! And yet, just hours after walking on campus for the first time, I somehow knew this was exactly where God was calling me. One of my favorite classes my first year was "Preaching 1" with Hulitt Gloer. Even though I still couldn't see myself as a pastor at the time, I knew that everything about this class filled my soul. One day Dr. Gloer prayed a simple yet profound prayer that we might hear what God wanted us to hear, do what God wanted us to do, and become who God wanted us to be. His prayer became my own and breathed new life into me throughout my time in seminary.

Sand Spring Baptist Church, Georgetown College, and Truett Seminary were all significant landmarks that pointed me toward God's calling on my life. However, the reality is that I wouldn't be a pastor today without Calvary Baptist Church in Waco, Texas. I began serving at Calvary as minister to children near the start of my seminary career. (Ironically, I would not have been prepared for this kind of ministry position without the experiences I received at my church back home.) I was still uncertain of my calling but eager to be used by God, and I loved investing in the lives of children in our church and community.

Interestingly enough, affirming women in ministry was beautifully woven into the fabric of Calvary's DNA. About 10 years earlier Calvary had become the first Baptist church in Texas to call a female senior pastor: Julie Pennington-Russell, the same preacher I had met in Atlanta. And there were picketers in full force to welcome Julie and her family into the church on her first Sunday as pastor. Even though Julie was no longer the pastor at Calvary when I was there, she (and many other women) had paved the way for Calvary to be a place where I would be wholeheartedly encouraged in my calling.

I went on to intern with Julie at First Baptist Church in Decatur, Ga., for a semester near the end of my time in seminary. I began to realize that part of the reason it had been so difficult for me to envision myself as a pastor was because I had never seen someone who looked like me do what I felt called to do. I needed to see what it looked like, day in and day out, for a woman to be a pastor. That time with Julie inspired me to begin to dream about becoming a pastor in a way I hadn't experienced before—not with fear and uncertainty, but with a newfound spirit of excitement and hope.

When I graduated from seminary the next year Calvary called me to become the associate pastor, and I began to invest myself in many different facets of ministry, mission, and our life together. After preaching my first sermon at Calvary, we sang "Great Is Thy Faithfulness," and I cried tears of joy that God had brought me into this specific community of faith. Only God could have known that it was exactly where I needed to be. I thought I might be asked to preach once a year, but Calvary welcomed me to share during this sacred hour time and time again, offering words of encouragement and blessing each time.

There's a great line near the end of *The Wizard of Oz* when Dorothy asks Glinda how she will ever get back home to Kansas. Glinda smiles and says to her, "Dorothy, you don't need to be helped. You've had the power all along, my dear." With just three clicks of her ruby red slippers, Dorothy says, "There's no place like home," and magically transports herself all the way back home to Kansas.

In a way, that's what Calvary did for me. There came a point in my journey when I realized that, whether or not I could ever see myself as a pastor, the people of Calvary saw me as one of their pastors. They inspired me to imagine something I had never been able to see within myself. They helped me to realize that I had the power of the Spirit all along. For eight years they equipped and empowered me to be a pastor, but then they gave me the biggest gift they could have given me when they called me to be their senior pastor in the spring of 2018. Being a pastor isn't at all what I was seeking when I first came to Calvary; if I'm being honest, I was actually running away from it. However, like the little girl in the story, when I found my church at the corner of 18th and Bosque, that's when I found my way home.

Mary Alice Birdwhistell is the pastor of Calvary Baptist Church in Waco, Texas, where she has served in ministry for 10 years. Originally from Kentucky, she is a 2009 graduate of Georgetown College and a 2013 graduate of Baylor University's Truett Seminary. Mary Alice loves sharing life with a diverse community of people and spending time on her back porch.

The Grip and the Embrace

Ronnie Brewer

As I reflect on my call story, I have been surprised at how hard it is to articulate. This is probably because it is so personal, even mystical. So, I am framing my thoughts around a common theme that I believe is foundational for all Christian calling: We live out our Christian lives in both the grip and embrace of God.

In childhood, and indeed throughout my life, God's grip and embrace were first evident in my mom. Her constant grip has reminded me to follow Jesus, love everyone, trust God always, and do right. Her embrace has been just as clear and constant: You are loved, you matter, God forgives and has a very special place for you in the world. It occurs to me that before I had any other models in the world to follow, my mom was the first to firmly and lovingly guide me toward the call of God.

Ensley Baptist Church in Birmingham, Ala., my childhood church, also taught me about God's call, with loving adults.

The people at my church knew me and loved me. They also had high expectations for me, corrected me when I needed it (which was quite often), and took great joy in my uniqueness. I can still picture many of the good folks of Ensley Baptist, and I give thanks for their love and direction.

Thank you, Mrs. McKinney, for teaching me about missions. Thank you, Mr. Birch, for teaching Sunday School to 12-year-old boys, which had to be hard. Thank you, Bob Curlee, for showing me the humanity and humor of pastors. Thank you, Mrs. Sims, for letting a small boy join you in the kitchen before Wednesday night dinners to "sample" your homemade yeast rolls. Thank you, church, for loving me and teaching me the commitment of following Jesus.

As I started college life at the University of Montevallo, philosophy and religious thought were certainly not consuming me. But, as I look back, there were many questions I would ask and answer during those years: What are my values? What do I believe about God? What will be my vocation? Will I marry? Who am I, really?

During college my most important community was the Baptist Student Union. So many unique and special people entered my life and loved me, while also deepening my faith and discipleship. I look back and give thanks for my friend and campus minister Bob Ford, ever the faithful guide for the nuances of the Christian journey. Bob, as much as anyone in my life, helped me to embrace both the gift and the demand of following Christ.

I recall the night, alone in my Montevallo dorm room, that I embraced a calling to serve God as a minister. That call has gripped me for more than 42 years and embraces me still. Questions still come, but so many early basic questions about my life found an answer by saying yes to the call of God.

A chapter of my calling was to serve in campus ministry. During my 17 years as a campus minister I served at Alabama A&M in Huntsville (a historically black campus), the University of Alabama in Huntsville (a high-tech commuter campus), and the University of Alabama in Tuscaloosa. In each place I felt the challenge of relating to students from many distinct backgrounds and cultures, often feeling inadequate, yet always finding that God would undergird my calling, while using my uniqueness and best self.

A call to help plant a church in the Huntsville area came somewhat out of the blue. While a campus minister, I accepted the call to join a dozen people to help start Trinity Baptist Church in Madison. The invitation to serve as the pastor of that congregation was both exhilarating and terrifying. The risk was high, but ultimately, so was the reward. God sustained and blessed our time at Trinity in a way that, even still, stirs my understanding of calling. I served at Trinity two separate times: for three years as the church was established, and then later for 11 years. God's grip and embrace have never been more evident to me than during my journey with Trinity.

As I reflect on my call story, I am thankful for so much: my teachers at Southern Seminary, who gifted me with tools for this calling; life-long ministerial friends and peers who have supported the ups and downs of this calling; the love of my life, Janet (a Montevallo girl!), who has been my best friend and partner in this calling; the students and churches I have been called to serve. But most of all, there is the grip and embrace of God . . . always there. Truthfully, I would have no call story without that.

Ronnie Brewer served for 11 years as the Baptist campus minister at the University of Alabama. He is the founding pastor of Trinity Baptist Church in Madison, where he served two tenures. He retired as the senior pastor of First Baptist Church in Bristol, Va. He and his wife, Janet, live in Destin, Fla.

When the Call Comes as a Surprise

Lee Canipe

"When I look at your heavens, the work of your fingers, the moon and stars that you have established; what are human beings that you are mindful of them, mortals that you care for them?" (Ps. 8:3-4).

Rarely, it seems, do we recognize those decisive turning points in our lives when they actually happen. It's only in retrospect that they assume their true significance. Stroking our chins as we do so, perhaps, in a way that makes us feel wiser than we are, we look back and are able to say, "Ah, yes. *That's* when it all started."

I imagine that a lot of "call" stories are like this. Few, if any, of my colleagues in ministry ever had a dramatic, thunderbolt, Paul-en-route-to-Damascus moment. If any of my friends had told me a story like that, I think I'd remember it. Far more common is the frog-in-a-pot-of-slowly-boiling-water type of call story, where the minister-to-be looks around one day and realizes that something's going on and she's suddenly got a choice to make: Either stay in the pot and let the Lord finish the job or jump out and remain forever partially cooked. Every story, though, has to start somewhere. And since mine is more of the frog-in-a-pot variety, I suppose I can look back, stroke my chin, and locate *a* moment, if not *the* moment, when it all started between the Lord and me.

Perhaps I was on a boat, in the middle of a lake, near the Swiss city of Lucerne. Alpine peaks towered all around the water's edge. It was one of those perfectly blue sky, impossibly clear fall days, and I remember looking at the mountains and hearing myself think, "I want my time on this earth to matter. I want to spend my life serving the God who made all this." That was it—a flicker of spiritual insight that went nearly as fast as it came.

But it never went away entirely. I was in Lucerne because what I'd really wanted to do during that fall semester of my junior year in college didn't work out. It was a bitter disappointment, and yet that disappointment, in a roundabout way, put me in a position to respond to God's majesty on that fall morning in Switzerland. What captured my imagination, and still holds it tightly even now, almost 30 years later, was the awe I felt in the presence of the God who made all of this beauty around me.

Ever since then—maybe even before that, but I can't be certain—the most important spiritual question for me, the one that has guided, strengthened, and sustained my faith, has been *Who?* Who made all this? Who loves me? Who can I trust? Who is the source of all truth and goodness? Who speaks to my soul and invites me to step out further than I can see? That morning, in Switzerland, I knew that the answer was God and that, for my life to matter, it would have to be spent somehow serving God.

That said, I had no intention of serving the God who made all this by serving the church. I had my reasons. For as long as I can remember, I've had a slight stutter, so the idea of getting up in front of a congregation and preaching a sermon every Sunday seemed like a stretch. Moreover, even if I managed to talk in a coherent manner, I seriously doubted that I could come up with anything interesting to say week after week. Preaching aside, I didn't want to deal with all the complaining that churches tend to generate, especially about things that are not, as the apostle Paul said, of "first importance" (1 Cor. 15:3). I liked having my weekends free. And the style I would be expected to pull off as a Baptist preacher in the South? I was too cool to wear a Ten Commandments tie, an Isaiah 40:31 belt buckle, and black dress sneakers. But I wasn't cool enough to wear mock turtlenecks, sport a goatee, and put gel in my hair. I could easily go on, but the point is: I had no desire to be a pastor.

Yet, still I felt that tug—the one from that day in Lucerne—and understood that, one way or another, I was going to have to reckon with it. I had professors in college who were top-notch economists, scientists, and so forth. They also sang in the choir, served as ushers, and filled leadership positions in the church there on campus. That impressed me. These professors obviously were dedicated Christians. They approached their respective disciplines from a perspective that was informed by their faith, and they taught impressionable students like me to do the same. They were, in their way, serving God, but it seemed to me they were doing it undercover. As college professors who got every weekend (and entire summers, plus three weeks at Christmas) off, they didn't have to put up with whiny church members, and they could use the same lecture notes year after year. I already had plenty of khakis and tweed jackets in my closet. The speaking in public part would still have to be finessed, but at least I had a plan: I would serve the God who made all this by being a history professor.

It didn't work out. As Jonah, the minor prophet, can attest, things rarely do work out like they're supposed to when God is pulling us in one direction and we're determined to go the other way. After a grim year or so of pulling in the opposite direction—or, as the King James Version of Acts 9:5 puts it, "kicking against the pricks"—I finally listened to a wise, retired pastor who suggested that I give divinity school a shot. "If it's not for you," he said, "you can always quit." Even after I had decided to try divinity school, but before I actually did, I still wasn't comfortable with the idea of becoming a minister. I now know that—all my aforementioned good reasons aside—my biggest problem was that I was afraid. Specifically, I was afraid of what others might think about my decision, afraid that they might think I'd gotten too big for my britches, that I believed I was somehow worthy of standing in the place of Moses and speaking God's word to God's people. The fact that I felt just the opposite only sharpened my anxiety.

I remember sitting at Smith Reynolds Airport in Winston-Salem one night with the late Ed Christman, longtime chaplain at Wake Forest. I was unburdening myself to him. I feel called to serve God through the church, I told him (a big concession on my part), but I'm having trouble explaining it to people. Rather than answer me directly, Ed told me about his own experience with the same struggle and how he dealt with one persistent friend who kept demanding an explanation for why in the world Ed would abandon a promising law career to enter the ministry.

"Why did you get married?" Ed asked him. After each proffered reason—love, companionship, security, and so on—Ed would fire back, "Well, yeah, but you don't have to be married to get that." Finally, the poor guy blurted out, "I can't explain it, but it just felt like the right thing to do!" With that, Ed looked at me and said: "And that's how you've gotta' be, brother. Trust God to do the right thing. You don't have to explain it to anyone else." Ed's words remain, perhaps, the best spiritual counsel I've ever received.

Time and again, throughout my experience as a Christian called to serve the God who made all this by serving God's church, I have only (and I do mean *only*) been able to step out in faith because I trust God to do the right thing. My faith is not in the what, how, why, where, or when. It's in the Who. If I get that right, then these more vexing (and, for me, frightening) questions tend to be resolved in a way that confirms my faith. Indeed, some of my greatest joy as a Christian has come in saying yes to God without having any answers to those how, why, where, or when questions—and then watching with amazement and gratitude as God works it all out.

When I am anxious, when I am discouraged, when I am scared, when I wrestle with doubt or am in the midst of those awful seasons of waiting for something that I can't put my finger on but I know is out there, what I hang on to with deep reverence and determined hope is my faith in the God who revealed himself to us in Jesus Christ; a God who is great enough to create the Alps, yet humble enough to become weak for my sake; a God who I can trust to take care of my life, both now and forever, and make sense of what I cannot understand. For, as I have come to believe, "neither death, nor life, nor angels, nor rulers, nor things present, nor things to come, nor powers, nor height, nor depth, nor anything else in all creation, will be able to separate us from the love of God in Christ Jesus our Lord" (Rom. 8:38-39). Because I know Who loves me, I can trust that this promise is true. Because I trust that this promise is true, I can offer my life in service to the God who made all this, if that's what the Lord requires of me.

In his *Poetics*, Aristotle wrote that good stories are a lot like ropes that gradually get tied up in ever-more complicated knots. When the knot is at its most knotty, it's hard to remember exactly how it got that way—and it's even harder to imagine how in the world it can ever be untied. But, in a good story the knot gets untied in just the right way and at just the right pace so that, once the rope is completely unknotted again, it's almost impossible to believe that things could have happened any differently than they did. A good call story is like that. Indeed, things could have been different for me at multiple points along the way from there to here, but, by the grace of God, they weren't. And for that, I am grateful—though, still, I'll confess, also a bit surprised.

Lee Canipe is the senior pastor of Providence Baptist Church in Charlotte, N.C. Before going to Providence, he served 12 years as the pastor of Murfreesboro Baptist Church in North Carolina. Lee and his wife, Hilary, have a daughter, Helen, and two sons, Watt and Peter.

When I Sensed That Mysterious Call to Ministry

Travis Collins

When I was a little boy, I'd come home from the worship service, stand at the coffee table in our living room, and preach. I'd try to remember the words the pastor had used that morning. In my childhood church we only used the King James Version of the Bible. So, I remember using the KJV phrase, "Verily, verily," a lot. I didn't know what "verily" meant, but it sounded extremely ministerial.

I almost always would give an invitation, an "altar call." My mother would come from the kitchen where she was preparing Sunday lunch, and my dad would get up out of his easy chair to "come forward." (My mom and dad must have held the world record for conversion experiences.)

Years later, when I was 20 years old, I was sitting with a pastor and his wife at Sunday lunch when I commented, "There is a part of me that would really enjoy being a pastor, but that's not what I'm going to do." He answered, "Wanting to be a pastor is not natural. You'd better be careful; that might be what God will call you to be."

The idea that I'd be a pastor one day, however, was fleeting. What I really thought is that I would be a minister of music. I loved singing from as far back as I could remember. As a 16-year-old, I directed the summer staff choir at Shocco Springs Baptist Camp in Talladega, Ala., and it was that summer that I sensed the call to what we used to describe as "full-time Christian service." As a 17-year-old, I became the "song leader" at our church. (We were a simple congregation with song leaders—not ministers of music—and songbooks, not hymnals.)

So, when I sensed that mysterious call to ministry, I was sure it was to a ministry in music. What I hadn't counted on, however, was how poor I would be at music theory. Upon my completion (barely) of Music Theory II, I abandoned my music major. I assumed that was the end of my call to ministry. I reasoned that I had misunderstood God.

Then, I came down the stairs from the cafeteria in Samford University's student center after lunch one day. At the bottom of the stairs a professor stopped me and asked, "Are you Travis Collins?" If you had known me when I was in college, you would know that it was not necessarily a good thing for a professor to be looking for me. With some trepidation, I admitted that I answer to that name.

The professor introduced himself as Dr. Bill Cowley. For two years (my junior and senior years of college), he took me to lunch, invited me to his home, mentored and challenged me, pulled no punches with me, and gently nudged me toward the two-year Missionary Journeyman program of the Southern Baptist Foreign Mission Board. It was nothing less than an act of God that Dr. Cowley introduced himself to me at the bottom of that staircase. His observation of me—of something I didn't see in myself—set me on my God-planned course.

When Dr. Cowley asked me what I was going to do upon graduation, I had no particular answer. I assumed I would be returning to my hometown to sell insurance or real estate. I decided to follow his suggestion to be a Journeyman for the simple reason that I didn't have anything better to do. No, it wasn't an especially "spiritual" decision. I figured it sounded like something good to do in two "meantime" years of my life. I could delay my real estate or insurance career for a couple of years.

I was 22, in Venezuela, when I had a mystical experience that I remember vividly. I was crossing a wide street, heavy with traffic, in downtown Caracas. Somewhat similar to—albeit less dramatic than—Paul's experience on the Damascus road, I had an awakening. It hit me: "There aren't many people who love this kind of life like I do." And with that came a deep and moving sense of rightness. I was immediately certain that I'd been called by the Creator to enjoy other cultures and languages and be some kind of missionary. Literally between the sidewalk on one side of the wide and treacherous street, and the sidewalk on the other side, my life had taken a new direction. I knew God had called me—wired me, prepared me, and set my heart ablaze—for cross-cultural ministry.

By age 24, I was back in the States, married to my college sweetheart who also sensed a call to international missions, and in seminary. In seminary I fell in love with learning for the first time and ended up attaining a Ph.D. in the study of missions. Within three months of my graduation we were in Nigeria immersed in the study of the Yoruba language, then teaching in a seminary and living a wonderfully fulfilling life.

During our first furlough, with our den filled with clothes and materials we had bought to return to Nigeria, my father had a massive and debilitating stroke. I am an only child, so my wife and I made the decision not to return to Nigeria so that we could care for my mother.

When we couldn't return to Nigeria, I accepted the call to be the pastor of another wonderful congregation—First Baptist Church of Mount Washington, Ky. After six years there I became pastor of another wonderful congregation—Bon Air Baptist, in Richmond, Va..

About a year before I became Bon Air Baptist's pastor, that church launched a Celebrate Recovery group—a ministry to people in recovery from addiction. That ministry quickly grew beyond the original model and became a new form of church that we named "Northstar." We had not yet heard the term, "fresh expressions of church," but that is what Northstar was. It was a new form (fresh expression) of church among a micro-culture (recovery community) and for people highly unlikely to walk into any church building you and I know.

Soon, a couple in Bon Air Baptist launched another fresh expression of church—a house church (which became a network of house churches) for immigrants. It was wildly successful. Then, we began a fresh expression (new form) of church for prostitutes.

Because of my experience in that church, and the new forms of church it launched, I was invited to join the Fresh Expressions U.S. Team.

Frankly, though Bon Air Baptist was a fine church, and really exciting things happened there, I was tired. I had walked up to the edge of burnout a couple of years earlier. Though I survived that brush with burnout, and had grown to love church leadership again, I was worn out. This new role serving the church-at-large, and getting a break from the weight of the pastorate, was a welcomed new opportunity.

My involvement in Fresh Expressions was like a return to my missions calling. The study of indigenous churches, the fact that North America is a "mission field," the opportunity to engage people far from God and not just attract dissatisfied members from other churches—all of that is part of this Fresh Expressions movement, and it enabled me to live out that cross-cultural missions calling I'd experienced so many years earlier.

The Fresh Expressions movement emphasizes the importance and potential of both inherited churches and new forms of church. On the one hand, it helps existing churches decide against helplessness in the face of change. It's about congregations with a great history deciding to have a great future of Kingdom investment.

On the other hand, the Fresh Expressions movement is encouraging and enabling "pioneers"—people with an apostolic gifting and a love for God and people—to follow God's call into innovative ventures. A fresh expression of church is simply a new form of church for a changing world, intended to reach people who need Jesus and who are highly unlikely ever to walk through the doors of a church.

Being a member of the Fresh Expressions U.S. Team was a great fit for me, a missionary-pastor.

While a full-time member of the Fresh Expressions U.S. team, I became the interim preacher at the First Baptist Church of Huntsville, Ala. I'd fly into Huntsville on Saturdays, preach on Sundays, and fly home Sunday evening or early Monday morning. It was delightful. For one thing, getting to preach without carrying the weight I'd carried as a pastor was like the best of both worlds. And my position with Fresh Expressions was just right for me. I didn't have to make any decisions. I simply wrote (two books about Fresh Expressions) and went to speak where I was told by the national director.

Furthermore, I fell in love with the people of First Baptist, Huntsville. They had been led by terrific pastors, were healthy and strong, had a sweet fellowship, and they loved on me. My wife, Keri, began accompanying me from time to time and fell in love with the people just as I had. When the good folks would ask why I didn't just become their pastor, I would give them a well-rehearsed answer: "I love my life with Fresh Expressions U.S., and I am called to serve there." Never did I give the slightest hint of my recurring, private thought: Being the pastor of this church would be so cool!

A trusted leader of the church drove me to the airport one day and said, "I want to give you some advice: This interim is going really well—so well that it is not going to be fair to the next pastor. If you serve up until the Sunday before the next pastor begins, then it's going to be really hard on everyone." His clear implication—that I should leave well before the interim ended—felt right to me.

So, when I was invited to be the interim preacher of a delightful congregation back in Richmond, I took it. Then, to make a long story short, I became the pastor of First Baptist Church of Huntsville six months later! And I am having the time of my life!

I still am a member of the Fresh Expressions U.S. team, helping out with them from time to time. And our church already has launched three fresh expressions of church—in the recovery community, the arts community, and in a disadvantaged neighborhood. We are, as I write this, on the cusp of a fresh expression of church among gamers.

As has been said often, "The will of God is best viewed in reverse." Sitting where I am now, looking back on 42 years of ministry (if you go back to my days as a teenaged song leader), I count myself more than blessed. The call—that stirring in my heart as a 16-year-old camp staff choir director that made me feel pretty sure I should be a vocational minister—has unfolded in ways I could not have imagined.

Travis Collins is the senior pastor of the First Baptist Church in Huntsville, Ala. He previously served as an international missionary, and is currently a member of the Fresh Expressions USA team. In addition to his ministerial responsibilities Travis enjoys playing golf and officiating high school football.

In Gladness and Brokenness

Matt Cook

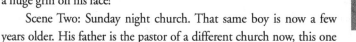

Scene One: A preschool room at a small church. Kids are laughing, playing and running—well, at least one of them is running. A little boy who just happens to be the son of the preacher has taken a few of those old cardboard boxes that look like bricks that every church used to have. He has set a few of them in a circle, and he is running as fast as he can, hurtling them as he goes. He is as fast as the wind, and there is a huge grin on his face!

Scene Two: Sunday night church. That same boy is now a few years older. His father is the pastor of a different church now, this one located in a big city. His mother has stayed home that night because she is sick, but the boy *wants* to go to church. And so, when they get to church his father asks him if he wants to sit on the podium with him. When they walk up the steps together, the boy's heart is beating 100 miles an hour. He's nervous and he wants to make sure that he doesn't do anything wrong (like yawn during father's sermon), but most of all he is excited.

Scene Three: The boy is now a young man. He has been asked to serve as the youth week pastor, which means he will be preaching a sermon. He works long and hard to preach well, but it's likely no one will remember that night's sermon but him. "We are therefore Christ's ambassadors, as though God were making his appeal through us!" The thought will stick with him, however, long after everyone else will likely have forgotten, a thought that is both fascinating and intimidating. "Speaking for God is an awesome responsibility…"

Scene Four: The young man is now a junior in college and is standing in front of his church. He has just spent his summer working at a Christian youth camp. He has had jobs before, but they were just *jobs*. But that summer spent working with teenagers, talking about God, never felt like that. He felt like a wide receiver must feel when he catches a winning touchdown, or like a cardiac surgeon when she repairs someone's heart. He felt like he was the best version of himself as he planned worship and taught the Bible and counseled teenagers. And now that the summer is over, he is standing in front of his church to tell them he thinks he is called to ministry.

Scene Five: The boy who became a young man who felt called is now a pastor. Some days are amazing. He loves to preach and help people discover more about Jesus. Some days are hard. A man in his church dies of a heart attack while he's out taking care of his yard. Most days fall somewhere in the middle. Some people are excited about what God is doing in their lives; other people are anxious because they remember a time when more people came to church.

Sometimes people even take their fears and frustrations out on that boy who became a young man who is now their pastor. But that too is part of the call.

"Calling," writes Frederick Buechner, "is the place where your deep gladness and the world's hunger coincide." I probably don't have to tell you that the young man in each of those scenes is me, or that somewhere in there was a moment where my calling began, even if I couldn't tell you then or now when that moment came. There are a handful of folks who have an overwhelming moment where God makes it clear what they're supposed to do, but I have yet to see a burning bush. Looking back, though, what I can see is a deep gladness that flows through me in the work of the church and its engagement with the world.

Much of that gladness has taken the shape of people who have blessed me and shaped me. My parents are people of deep and abiding faith. Their faith isn't showy, but it has stood the tests of time and occasional trials. My father is a pastor and would tell you quickly how blessed his life in ministry has been and that is true even when the underbelly of the church has showed itself in certain moments, and his experience has shaped my own. The call is almost always modeled *for* us before it is extended *to* us.

Looking back, I'd also add that my youth minister Tony Rankin had a significant impact on my sense of calling. He took the Bible seriously, but just as importantly he took us teenagers seriously. I think it's easy for the children of ministers to take faith for granted because the trappings of faith are so commonplace in a minister's home. Tony helped me develop a faith that was my own and gave me my first real opportunities to use my giftedness and leadership skills.

Other mentors have shaped me as well. In college Bill Leonard was my boss (I was his student assistant), but he was also a friend and intellectual guide; I'm not sure I'll ever have a class that shaped me more than reading Kierkegaard with Dennis Sansom; and Chip Conyers, my theology professor at Truett, may be the reason I'm still a minister (and a Christian for that matter) today. I had transferred to Truett Seminary from Southwestern Baptist Theological Seminary in the aftermath of the firing of Russell Dilday, and I was filled with a white-hot anger toward all things fundamentalist. Dr. Conyers gently helped me to see that while the issues that divided Baptists did matter, I shouldn't construct my theology, or conceptualize ministry, in the context of such bitterness.

In addition to my mentors, I would add the gladness that friends and colleagues have contributed. Sustaining a call to ministry is impossible without the deep gladness that friends reveal and amplify in us. There are too many stories to tell here about the insights that friends have shared that shaped me as a minister. Nor is there space for the moments when I would have walked away from the ministry without the sustaining love they've given freely.

Each of these relationships has been critical to the process of discovering and sustaining my call. I learned to love preaching because I heard good preaching. My father was and is a gifted preacher, but being the son of a preacher gave me both an awareness and an appreciation of a variety of gifted preachers. While I was at Truett, Baylor University released the first of its surveys on the most gifted preachers in the English language and then brought a number of those preachers to campus. Not only hearing ministers such as Barbara Brown Taylor and Will Willimon preach, but also having the opportunity to peek behind the curtains of their preparation and ask them questions one-on-one was a rare and wonderful gift. In that way, their deep gladness contributed to my own.

I have also been energized repeatedly by the most creative ministers among us. Much of the way I think about the church's need for greater creativity can be traced to the mad scientist's laboratory environment that characterized the six years I spent working with a team of college and seminary students in my youth camp days. For me, being creative was essential to my sense of calling as it developed, and it continues to be essential in these days when mindless habits and tired programs must give way to the adaptive leadership required when ministers and churches find themselves in unexplored territory.

Most of the scenes I've described come out of gladness—moments of joy or passion or both. But calling, at least according to Buechner, is not simply a matter of discovering our deep gladness but also of discovering "the world's hunger." Hunger is a good word, but too much hunger can make people scared or angry. Sometimes I wonder if we should substitute the word "brokenness" for hunger, if we're going to understand what it means to be called.

In the early years of my calling, I might have avoided such an insight. It is far easier to celebrate the ways in which calling is planted in the soil of friendship or expressed in our gifts and strengths than it is to acknowledge that a call to ministry is a call to pick up a cross and carry it. I wrotfe part of that last scene as a kind of amalgamation of some of my hardest moments in ministry. Suffering alongside people is hard. When they hurt, we hurt. I am writing this just a few days after a man in my church died just weeks after he had retired (and only in his mid 60s), and later tonight I will sit alongside his widow as we study the Bible together. Tomorrow I will visit another man who has spent most of the last 18 months in and out of the hospital. That is hard.

Even harder is when their pain, whatever is causing it, becomes a weapon that they wield on us. If ministry is the place where our deep gladness wells up, it is also the place where we are confronted powerfully with the brokenness of people, and sometimes that brokenness has a jagged edge that draws blood. But as hard as that may be on us occasionally, I have come to realize that in its own way that is among the most powerful indications of our calling.

In the first church where I served as a pastor there was a man who almost overnight became one of my biggest critics, and for reasons that made no sense—at least to me. Thankfully, I was blessed in that church with a friend and mentor who had nearly 40 years of pastoral experience. We went to lunch one day and in the middle of some food Mexican food and a lot of laughter he asked me about this man. I unloaded. I let all my hurt and frustration out because I knew I could trust my friend. He listened knowingly. He had been there too. But then he told me something that has stuck with me ever since: "Matt, before you take all that personally you might carefully ask around. I have often found that people who are the biggest problems in church are in a lot of pain at home even if they might not see it that way." I checked and he was right. The man had a situation with one of his adult children that was incredibly difficult and because he couldn't control that situation, he was lashing out in other areas of his life including at church.

If you want to know if you're called to ministry, then look around for the places and the people in which your gladness wells up most easily. Look for things that others might see as work, but that you see as something you feel blessed to do. But don't just look in the bright sunshine of your gladness; look also in the shadow of others' brokenness. Calling may be born in the sunshine of our gladness, but my own experience has taught me that it is confirmed in the shadow of human brokenness.

As for me, there's a part of me that realizes I am still that same child running around the church. I am still trying to leap hurdles, and, on most days, I have a grin on my face. Thanks be to God!

Matt Cook has served as a pastor in churches in Texas, Arkansas, and North Carolina. He is married to Allyson, and they have two children, Nathaniel and Caroline. He currently serves as the senior pastor of First Baptist Church of Wilmington, N.C.

Living Into My Calling

Patrick DeVane

"Doug! Doug! Come here! The knives in the play kitchen work! They open the doors! We can pick all the locks in this building with the knives from the play kitchen!"

The rhythm of church frames my life from my earliest memories . . . every Sunday, every Wednesday, summers in Vacation Bible School, Sunday School every week. We were active, happy, and excitedly part of a growing church. I became best friends with the pastor's son, Doug, and, since my father ran the sound system for worship each week, Doug and I often wound up in the church buildings without others around.

I remember sensing a sacredness there that I found invigorating. There was something wonderful and interesting about the sanctuary and classrooms sitting silent and empty, as if in anticipation of some gathering but not yet ready to occur. I wound up exploring the church often with Doug each week before and after service. We would find whatever trouble we could—including successfully picking the locks in the brand-new children's building using plastic knives.

This was the frame of my life. I enjoyed a happy family, good friends, and a great church. I made a profession of faith in the second grade and, when the congregation came up to congratulate me, so many people were excited for me that my glasses bent out of shape from all the bear hugs. Everything was in harmony, and I was naively happy. Then conflict and controversy suddenly sprang up in the church. Before I could understand what was happening, my family found itself suddenly on the outside looking in, with former friends and fellow congregants now shunning us. While officially I was still welcome at the church, in reality, we were thrown out. I had just started the fifth grade. I felt betrayed and disillusioned.

I began middle school grieving my losses, angry at God, and facing the changes in me and my life absent the safety and connection of church. Faith and church were fused in my heart and my mind. While I knew I could still pray and that God still loved me, I hardly saw the point in engaging if the end result was me becoming like the people who had hurt me. In the wisdom I had gained in my 13 years, I loudly declared that if God allowed this to happen then that was no God worth serving. While my words were sure and boastful, my heart had questions and grief. Out of answers and struggling to make sense of my situation, I would secretly pray each night begging for guidance and help. I had been taught all my life that God was always near, and yet God seemed silent during these years. I refused to let anyone see or know about these prayers, adamantly maintaining my aloofness and disregard for faith.

This was how my life continued until high school began. The summer before high school my mother sat down with me and stated: "We bought a trumpet many years ago. Both of your brothers played this trumpet. You are now going to be in the marching band and play the trumpet too." That was the end of the discussion.

My freshman year of high school was dominated by marching band experiences. One of the formations of our program called for the trumpet players to march between the clarinet players. During one of the many breaks in practice, I began talking with the clarinet player standing next to me. I really liked her and, working up all the courage I had, I asked if I could spend more time with her. She said that she spent each morning before school at the Fellowship of Christian Youth (FCY). The next morning, I was the first one waiting outside of the faculty sponsor Mrs. Ingle's door to join this group.

The FCY was a student-led group that sang praise songs and had a short devotional message each morning before school began. I had come to the group to try and woo a girl, but, in the process, I found myself being wooed back by God. I was hooked on the music and the familiar cadences, stories, and rhythms of regular worship. This felt like home and began feeding a part of my soul that had languished for years.

I started going to FCY each morning. I could not get enough of it. I began dating the clarinet player only to discover that her father was a pastor. Soon, I was attending services with her and her family. My faith became a loud and prominent feature in my life again. I was overwhelmed with Jesus. I read the Bible for at least an hour each day, took copious notes during sermons and Bible studies, and talked to whomever I could about life and faith issues.

Over the next few months I began helping to lead FCY. I would coordinate speakers and help plan music with the other leaders, and it all felt so natural. In the spring of my freshman year we were instructed in one class to begin thinking about what we would want to choose for our careers. We were told to think of something where our passion and talents could meet. I spent a long time thinking about that concept. I was passionate about learning. I loved to read, and I had always loved school, but I also wanted to help people. I wanted to give, to serve, and to do something that could match my love of learning with my love of helping people.

One night, as I was praying and asking God what I needed to do with my life, the answer came in a clear voice in my head. It was audible, distinct, and unlike anything I had experienced before. I knew instantly it was God. The voice said simply, "Ministry." I had never imagined being a minister. I didn't really know anything about what ministry entailed, but I had a peace and assurance that this is what I was meant to do.

The next morning, I went into FCY and signed up for the next available slot to speak to the group, a day two weeks away. If I was called to be a minister, here was a group that I could share my gifts with immediately. This seemed the perfect setup, and I spent the next two weeks in feverish preparation trying to make sure that everything was perfect for my first lesson. I had an easily available model to follow. My friend Johnny was one of the other leaders of the group. He also felt led to ministry and was a recurring speaker at FCY. He was funny and a great communicator. I knew that I could do that too.

When the big day came, I was confident and ready. As I started my talk, the adrenaline surged through my body. I was ecstatic. I was doing it. I was leading a group. Then, I hit a wall. No one was laughing at the jokes I had carefully crafted. No one smiled or even seemed interested in what I was saying. The Holy Spirit did not fall upon those gathered, revival did not break out, and, even worse, no one even seemed to be paying attention. When I was done, I prayed and then there was a deafening silence as everyone gathered up their things and quickly left the room. I was devastated. This never happened to Johnny. If I could not grab the attention of this group that I knew, maybe I misunderstood the call to ministry.

I was despondent and was slowly gathering my things to leave when Mrs. Ingle came up to me and said that she was proud of what I had said. I told her that I did not think it had gone well at all and was wondering if maybe I had misunderstood the meaning of the voice that night. She locked eyes with me and said, "Not everyone is called to talk to teenagers. Johnny can do that really well. You just gave a talk that adults in my church need to hear. You need to talk to adults. If God has called you to ministry, nothing can stop you."

After high school I enrolled at Samford University in Birmingham, Ala. I initially majored in history, thinking the smart thing to do in case ministry did not work out was to have something sensible on which to fall back. The plan was to become certified to be a history teacher and then go to seminary. Within the first week of classes I knew I had made a mistake. I wanted to study religion and had for years. I dropped my classes, changed my major, and prayed desperately that God would cover me if I made this choice.

Both undergraduate religion studies and seminary provided me the educational background I needed for ministry. I am grateful for the classes, the rigor, the friendships, and my own growth that occurred in these settings. What I did not understand at the time was how I was allowing my studies to shape my definition of call and ministry. Without making a conscious decision to do this, I came to believe that if I was an excellent student, then I would be an excellent minister. I equated academic rigor with ministerial faithfulness. I neglected my own spiritual journey and underestimated the importance of relational wisdom and emotional intelligence. My arrogance was only matched by my perfectionism. I refused to give myself, or anyone else, grace. God demanded perfection, I came to believe, and so should I.

My first congregation suffered through my attempts to turn them into a perfectionist mini-seminary. As the pastor, I felt it was my responsibility to take the important lessons I had learned in class and educate these congregants. One example of my misguided educational efforts was trying to explain nine different types of psalms in one 50-minute Bible study. Everything in my mind was going well, until suddenly I hit another wall.

Three years into this first pastorate, I went through a difficult divorce. Faced with an uncertain future and shattered dreams, I could no longer cling to perfectionism, and the academic rigor I had preached rang hollow in my ears. It was then that my congregation rose up around me and taught me about faithfulness, grace, and mercy. When I finally couldn't hide my own brokenness, they modeled for me lessons of stability and community that have shaped how I've served every congregation since. They taught me as much about ministerial excellence as my many years of higher education, and I am profoundly grateful for them.

As I continue to embrace and wrestle with my call to ministry, I find that when I bring all of myself to my ministry, I find the most joy and the deepest response from others. When I am honest and open, others open up themselves. When I allow my congregation to see my struggles and my triumphs, they are eager to share their own as well. God has used every triumph and failure in my life and all the moments inbetween in my ministry.

My call is no longer a burden or an intimidating standard demanding perfect performance; it is, instead, a joy and a gift that I treasure. It is interwoven into every part of my life, and I rejoice that I get to honor and live into my call to ministry for the rest of my life. From picking locks to picking up the pieces after my life had fallen apart, God has blessed me beyond measure each step of the way with a calling that continues to draw me closer to Jesus Christ so that I can share what I see with everyone I know.

Patrick DeVane is the senior pastor of College Parkway Baptist Church in Arnold, Md. He loves reading, playing board games, and spending time with his family.

Nurtured by the Church

Doug Dortch

I am a child of the church. I can't remember a time in my life when I wasn't being nurtured by some local congregation of Christians—a gift that continues to this present day.

My faith journey began at the First Baptist Church of Chickasaw, Ala., a bedroom community of Mobile. FBC Chickasaw was a large church that offered every children's ministry imaginable, all of which I enthusiastically attended. Those ministry activities gave me the opportunity to learn not only of Christ's love for me but also of his purpose for me. That purpose, though not confined to vocational ministry, certainly was held up in that church as a distinct possibility to which every believer should be open. Even in those early years, I took that invitation most seriously so that the fulfillment I felt as a child immersed in church activities moved me to consider a future in congregational ministry work as the most natural and exhilarating future I could know.

When my parents moved to a small town in West Alabama, I was fortunate to find in my new community a similarly encouraging local church that offered opportunities for me to continue to explore God's call upon my life. My new church, York Baptist Church, invested heavily in youth ministry and I reaped the spiritual dividends from that investment. While the awkwardness of adolescence certainly factored into my understanding of God's call, and I wasn't fully certain of much of anything during that season of life except my commitment to Christ, my church's patient love and support kept the prodding of the Spirit alive in my soul.

It was my college experience that solidified my understanding of God's call to vocational ministry. During those formative years I found other students at the local Baptist Student Union who were seeking clarity in the same ways. Moreover, my college church, University Baptist of Montevallo, Ala., gave me space not only to grow in my worship life, but also to process my questions about faith's intersection with higher learning, which expanded my understanding of where God's call to ministry might actually take me.

In particular, an opportunity that came my way the summer of my freshman year in college enabled me to put my faith to the test. During a break on a BSU ministry trip, my college pastor stepped on the bus as we were about to head out and made an announcement that would change my life. He had just received a call from a pastor friend whose church was looking for a college student to be their summer youth minister. It was a 10-week commitment to guide a group of high school students in the same way that a college student had guided me during my high school years. As the pastor invited us to speak with him if we felt any interest in the position, I sensed the Spirit nudging me to look into that opportunity as a way to see if I had the gifts and abilities to serve in such a way.

That summer with the First Baptist Church of Vernon, Ala., was all of the confirmation I needed as to God's call to vocational ministry. The joy I felt in helping young people draw nearer to Jesus, many of whom were not much older than I, gave me a deep confidence that doing this type of work was God's purpose for my life. I returned to college that fall with a clear direction for which I needed to prepare. From that time on, I looked for every opportunity to sharpen my skills and soften my heart so that I might be able to be used for Christ's cause to the best of my ability.

The thread that runs through my story is the nurturing power of the local church and its ability to create a culture where the conditions for the Spirit's call are a part of everything the church does. I would not be where I am today if it were not for those grace-filled congregations that awakened, developed, and strengthened my faith. In each congregation there were, of course, individuals who stand out in my experience because of how they saw ministry possibilities in me that I would never have seen in myself. But beyond those persons, there was the larger community that simply went about their mission in quiet but steady faithfulness so that the Spirit had room to touch my heart as only the Spirit could do.

Those who read my story may be alert and sensitive to God's hand on some young man or woman in their churches and may have the gift of encouraging those young persons to consider the possibility of vocational ministry. If so, please take the time to broach such a possibility with them. It will be the best action you could take for them, for you, for your church, and, of course, for the cause of Christ.

For everyone else who is a part of a local congregation, simply know that what your church does week in and week out, in both its worship and service, are vehicles for the Holy Spirit to do his calling work. In the rhythms of church life, God's call is often discerned. So, go about your place in your church with enthusiasm and joy so that you may contribute to a culture of call where the local congregation becomes the nurturing influence that all of my churches were for me. Rest assured that some young person in your life will be better for your having done so, and, at the end of the day, so will the Kingdom of God.

Doug Dortch has been the senior minister of Mountain Brook Baptist Church in Birmingham, Ala., since 2011. Prior to this he served as the pastor of churches in Kentucky, Alabama, and Florida. A huge golf fan, he and his wife Judy have two adult children and two grandchildren. Doug is a past moderator of the Cooperative Baptist Fellowship.

Circles of Influence

Michael Duncan

I am the son of teachers. I come from a family of teachers. My aunts are teachers and have taught me. My uncles are teachers and have taught me. My friends' parents have been teachers and have taught me. A community of teachers has shaped me and played a definite role in my call. They have been the circle of influence in my life and upon my call.

During college my father did his student teaching with the mother of one of my best friends. She was pregnant with my friend during that time, and after she went into labor while my dad was working with her, he became her substitute. As he began his education career, my father also worked at the city pool in Jacksonville, Ala., where he oversaw operations. One of his employees taught me how to swim. That same employee became my first-grade teacher.

In her class I was a talkative child, and my social nature reinforced my comfort level in her classroom. When I got in trouble and was sent to my desk while the rest of the class participated in story time, I experienced my first-ever memory of disappointing someone I loved and respected. To make matters worse, the principal chose that day to come to her classroom to check in. I had my head on my desk, and I knew that word was going to get back to my parents. It did, and that was the last time I found myself in trouble in that class, or in any other class for that matter, because the circle around me was tight.

Instead of feeling oppressed by the circle, I have been freed. I have been guided by an unspoken accountability to those around me. As I reflect now, I can trace back to that one instance the formation of self-determination and drive not to disappoint those I love and respect. It has guided my educational path inside and outside the classroom. It has also shaped my ministerial calling.

I was not raised in church. Like many children born and raised in the South, though, I attended my fair share of Vacation Bible Schools during the summers. I drank the Kool-Aid and ate the cookies. I played and made those paper crafts that were quickly lost, destroyed, or trashed. I heard the stories of God and Jesus and their love for me, but I never was pressured into making a decision to give my heart to Jesus. My heart and head had not yet come to an understanding of those matters. That came later, and the circle of influence was once again the motivator.

As I entered the sixth grade, a family friend invited me to church. He was a teacher who taught with one of my aunts and rented a house from my grandparents. The church of which he was a member was the church home of my maternal grandparents and great-grandparents.

I had aunts, uncles, and cousins in that church. They welcomed me, and I felt at home. The Bible stories I had heard as a young child started working on my heart and in my mind, and after what seemed like a long period of refusal and denial since I did not think myself worthy, I came to accept the love of Christ for me. I pledged my life to him and joined my family's church.

It was in that church, the First Baptist Church of Williams, Ala., that I learned how to pray. I was reminded of God's love each and every Sunday by good and loving teachers and pastors. I was challenged to deepen my faith, which was accomplished through daily quiet times, Bible study during Sunday School, Sunday night youth fellowships, and Wednesday night devotions. I was immersed in youth mission trips and summer choir tours. I was called upon to lead Sunday morning worship experiences and sang in the adult choir. My church was family, and the circle of influence grew.

One night during one of those youth studies, our youth director asked those in attendance who they saw as leaders within the group. After a time of nervous silence followed, he called out my name as one he saw as a leader. His words of affirmation and challenge planted a seed in my life. Continued service in the church watered that seed, and my role as a leader was confirmed when I was called to serve on a pastor search team as a youth. In college, involvement and service with the Baptist Campus Ministry nurtured the seed. Mission trips, Bible studies, worship experiences, and opportunities to lead fertilized the soil and fed the seed. Before it could sprout, however, life's other commitments took precedence.

My course of study was fast-tracked by my scholarship program. As an incoming freshman, I was already on a path to graduate in three years because the program required summer internships and coursework. In accepting the scholarship, I agreed to work for the government wherever it sent me. After graduation the doors opened locally for employment, which allowed me to stay at my home church. Through my service and involvement in the church, the seed of ministry began to sprout.

Since education was so important to me, I began to look at seminaries. I chose the one closest to my home, Mercer University's McAfee School of Theology in Atlanta, Ga. As with my previous educational experiences, I already had circles that existed for me at McAfee. God had also prepared other circles at Peachtree Baptist Church in Atlanta for me and others like me. During those seminary days Peachtree was dubbed "McAfee South." Seminary student after seminary student came through those halls. We loved on the people and were loved by them. They challenged us. They encouraged us. They taught us and even gave us space to teach. When we failed, they loved us through our lessons. When we succeeded and were called elsewhere, they offered blessings. It was there that this call to congregational church ministry bloomed and began to bear fruit.

My first call after seminary was to a little church in a little town in the south-central section of Virginia. Central Baptist Church and the town of Altavista welcomed me. They took a risk on me that few churches were willing to take. I was single. I was fresh out of seminary. Yet, they called, and I believed it was of God. I went there with no connections to the area.

I had a few contacts and friends in Virginia through my involvement with the Cooperative Baptist Fellowship but none in and around Altavista. I knew I needed a new circle, and God provided many.

The first circles were composed of ministers. The Altavista Area Ministerial Association and the pastors' conference of the Catawba River Baptist Association introduced me to seasoned pastors of varying theological perspectives and denominational traditions. Their presence, their words, and their examples inspired and challenged me in my work. The circles expanded to community agencies such as the boards of the local chapter of Habitat for Humanity and the YMCA. Those groups and many other community connections shaped me and prepared the soil for an extended call to the community. As that call shifted to the church I am currently serving, the circles guided me in my deliberation and discernment.

Today, I am grateful for the circles of my life. I am thankful for the circular path my life has taken as I teach, proclaim the good news, and serve God's people at Drexel First Baptist Church in North Carolina. I am indebted to the circle of countless faithful servants of God who have opened their lives and homes to me and shared faith with me. With a heart overwhelmed with an abundance of gratitude, I am mindful of each kindness and patient word of encouragement they have offered to me along this journey. I am ever hopeful that gratitude and faith guide the remainder of my ministry, and I look forward to the new circles that God has in store for me and others.

Michael L. Duncan Jr. is the pastor of Drexel First Baptist Church in Drexel, N.C. In addition to his church responsibilities, he is involved in a pastor's lectionary group and his local ministerial association. In his spare time he enjoys golf, travel, and a good story.

From Medical School to Ministry

Matt DuVall

Sometimes the way you think you will get there isn't actually the way you end up going.

I grew up in church. Except for a pretty long stretch in college, I don't remember a time when I wasn't in church. My parents were both dedicated lay leaders in our Baptist church in Cordele, Ga., where I grew up. We were there every time the doors were opened and we qualified for the program. We sang in children's and youth choirs and participated in RAs and GAs and Bible drills. My siblings and I all made professions of faith at young ages, and the expectation for all of us was that church activities came before all others. We could do anything we wanted, as long as it didn't interfere with church.

I was working one summer in my father's internal medicine practice. I sat at the front desk welcoming those who had come for appointments, scheduling and rescheduling new and future appointments, and generally trying to make the office run as smoothly and efficiently as possible. I had a personal incentive to make that happen: If my father finished his day early, we got to leave and go hit some balls on the golf course.

It was a normal Tuesday morning toward the end of June. I always glanced down at the schedule first thing to see if there would be any patients coming that day who I knew already, especially any fellow members of the First Baptist Church of Cordele. I always loved to see people I knew and spend some time visiting with them. There was only one familiar church name that Tuesday: the Judge. I knew that if the Judge came for an appointment, then Mrs. Doris would be there too, and I loved to talk with her.

You see, Mrs. Doris was one of those people who always wanted to know how you were doing. She had a twinkle in her eye and the warmest smile you ever saw. She was an avid outdoorswoman, a crack-shot, and still loved to go turkey hunting, even in her 70s. The Judge still had a brilliant legal mind, but his body would not cooperate as it once did because of a major stroke. However, with a village of support he was still able to perform his duties on the bench. My father, a close personal friend of the family in addition to being their physician, was always glad to spend extra time with the Judge to help him in his reduced state. Of course, that meant throwing off the timing of my expert scheduling, but it also meant I was able to spend more time talking with Mrs. Doris. I was always glad for that time.

We began our conversation that day talking about the Judge and how he was doing. Mrs. Doris filled me in on everything they had been working on in therapy and how she helped him to manage each day. As she went through their day in detail, I caught a glimpse of the weariness of the routine and the grief of what had been lost behind her smiling eyes. After she finished telling me about her husband's needs, she stopped. And then it happened. Somewhere down deep within me I heard a voice that said, "Ask her how she is doing." So, I did. "Mrs. Doris," I said, "Thank you for catching me up on the Judge, but I was also wondering how you are doing. I imagine this has taken quite a toll on you, too. How are you doing?"

She looked at me with those eyes that I have seen hundreds of times since—those eyes that say, "Thank you for asking." She relaxed her shoulders and began to slowly share what this had been like for her, how it had completely changed her life too, and how she was in deep grief about their diminished quality of life after the stroke. Before she had finished, the nurse came out and asked her to join her husband and my father in the exam room. We hugged, and she whispered in my ear, "You are really good at this." What a word of blessing!

For years I had known I wanted to help people. If you had asked me what I wanted to do with my life, I would have told you that I wanted to be in the medical field like both of my parents because that was the model I had seen most often for how to help people. In a way, that experience with Mrs. Doris reinforced my thinking because my interaction with her happened in a physician's office. There had been ministers, including my own youth minister whom I loved, who had suggested to me that I might consider ministry as an option. I did love being in church. I loved participating in church. I deeply loved and respected my grandparents who were ministers, and I had even wondered out loud with them what that work would be like, but as far as I was concerned at the time, the medical field was the direction I was headed. I had even gone so far as to declare pre-med as my major when I committed to attend Mercer University.

But then everything fell apart for me as I was finishing my senior year. My grandfather was in the hospital for routine surgery in Albany, Ga., and he never made it home. Our family was thrown completely off balance, as most families are when dying and death become part of their story. I did what all teenagers do, which was to call my friends. One of those friends I reached out to was someone just as involved in church as I was. Missy said that she and her sister, another dear friend, would come down for the visitation from college. She never made it. Missy and her boyfriend were killed in a wreck on their way to Macon from Athens. I was in shock. I was lost. I was overwhelmed. The world I had known was not the world I was now living in. I was looking for some kind of help, support, or space to process the deep pain I was feeling in those moments.

When I expressed my feelings to the leaders at my church, their response wasn't helpful. They said things like: "This was all a part of God's plan. You can't be sad because they are with Jesus. God only takes the best ones. God needed another flower for his garden. Just have faith." What should have been met with compassion and empathy, along with space for deep grief, reflection, silence, and mystery was met with Hallmark cards and cotton candy. I decided that I was sure I wouldn't have anything to do with an institution that had so little to offer to someone who needed so much.

And so, I went the other way, like Jonah fleeing from God's calling in his life. If Jonah spent three days in the belly of the beast before finally finding his way, I spent three years wrestling with my call at Mercer before finding my way. I remained in pre-med until I took organic chemistry, and then I changed my major to communications. What a disappointment. I struggled with what I was meant to do, and, at the same time, I deeply desired to please everyone around me. I was trying to find the one thing for me while also sampling everything that was in front of me. I avoided anything church-related and spent too much time in the wilderness even as I desired to be out of the wilderness. And then, finally, I was overcome with depression.

So, I left Mercer and went home with the hopes that I could finally find my way. It was one of the scariest and yet most freeing times in my life. I was finally able to admit that I needed help, and through many counseling sessions I found my way. As I was preparing to re-enter Mercer for my last year with an eye toward graduation and what would come after, I began to ask myself, "When was the last time I had a deep sense that I was doing something right?" And then I remembered Mrs. Doris.

I began to realize that I wanted to help people. I wanted to be a part of something that gave people the space to ask the deep and difficult questions we all face in life. I wanted to be a part of something that provided a steady and graceful presence to people. I wanted to be a part of a place that didn't abandon people in the midst of the struggle, but that walked alongside them and sat with them when they didn't know which end was up. I wanted to be a part of something that offered a word of blessing to people—a blessing that affirmed who they were and what they had to offer, rather than hammering them with what they did wrong and making them feel guilty for the mistakes they had made. In short, I wanted to be a part of something that would have been helpful and life-giving for me in what I had been through already in my life—something that I hadn't found but I was sure had to exist somewhere because I could imagine it.

A mentor told me that this something I was looking for could be called church. So, when I graduated from Mercer, instead of going into the medical field, I went on to the McAfee School of Theology to attain an MDiv degree so that I could be a part of this kind of church as a minister. What I have come to understand of late is that my calling never was to find that kind of church, but it was to become that kind of church, and to be the kind of minister that helps a church become that kind of church. And that calling continues to carry me through the rest of my life. Thanks be to God.

Matt DuVall is the pastor of the First Baptist Church of Rome, Ga. He has served churches in Georgia and Kentucky and has also served as a development officer for the McAfee School of Theology at Mercer University. He is married to Caroline Ross, and they have two daughters, Cate and Arly.

So That's How I Ended Up Being a Preacher

Jimmy Gentry

"So how did you end up being a preacher?" Over the course of more than 40 years in vocational ministry, I've been asked that question often. A few times, when I've been asked what my vocation was, and I've said that I'm a "pastor" or "preacher," the response has been "I'm sorry." To which I've gently, but firmly, said, "I'm not sorry!" I'm sure most of us in professional ministry have heard the "I pity you" reply in some form or another when someone learns of our vocation. But what a vocation it is!

The journey of my calling to ministry dates to early childhood. I can honestly say that I have always wanted to be a minister. Of course, there were other things I wanted to be, too. But I always came back to the minister thing.

Born and reared in the small town of Cadiz, Ky., I was most fortunate to be nurtured by loving parents who were believers. That nurturing was undergirded by the Cadiz Baptist Church where, for the first 12 years of my life, my pastor was J. Norman Ellis.

From the time I first came to really know "Brother Ellis" when I was a little boy, I was enthralled with him. This humble man had no hint of intimidation. Even as a child I realized he was intelligent and spiritually adept, loved people, and had an ability to see in others what they did not see in themselves. And I am thankful he saw something in me and told me what he saw. He told me shortly after he baptized me a month before my 10th birthday that he believed God was going to use me in ministry. He had no idea that I idolized him and wanted to be just like him. Or intuitive as he was, maybe he did.

As a child of seven or eight years old, I often played church in my room. I pretended I was Brother Ellis and led worship as if it were a Sunday morning. I literally preached sermons! Well, I preached something. I never told anyone I did this, but if someone asked what I enjoyed doing I would say, "I like to play church."

My father had been actively involved in the church as a deacon and song leader. He was also active in the local Baptist association in which served as treasurer. He was 65 years old when I was born. I idolized him, too. And like Brother Ellis, I wanted to be like my daddy for whom I was named. I figured "Being like Daddy and Brother Ellis, I can't go wrong!" When I was 12 my father died of a heart attack at age 78. It was a late Sunday afternoon, but Brother and Mrs. Ellis came to our home immediately after worship that evening. The next morning when my mother and I arrived at the funeral home, Brother Ellis was there waiting for us. He conducted my father's funeral on the Tuesday before Thanksgiving Day in 1968.

The following Sunday, Brother Ellis resigned to become the pastor of a church in Jackson, Tenn. I didn't understand why he was leaving, but my Sunday School teacher tried to explain.

In addition to what was happening in the nation, 1968 was a hard year for me personally. My dog, a black Lab named Flip that I had for more than six years, ran off and never came back. A few months later someone gave me another dog; Peggy Sue contracted distemper and was euthanized at three months. One of my best friends, Angela, moved to Washington, D.C. Another dear friend, Jeannie, saw her daddy killed as he was struck by a car. My daddy died. And Brother Ellis left. In all of this, I experienced a presence and strength that was beyond me.

On Brother Ellis' last Sunday as pastor, during the evening service, he called on me to say the closing prayer. I had no idea he was going to do that. I prayed for Brother and Mrs. Ellis, and for my church. As I have reflected on that grace Brother Ellis extended to me nearly 50 years ago, I acknowledge that it was one of the most touching moments of my life. He entrusted a 12-year-old with saying the final prayer of his 12-year tenure in that church. I've never forgotten that. He saw something in me, and I'm glad he did.

In April 1970 I went with some other junior high and high school students to Louisville, Ky., to hear a preacher who was pulling a wooden cross from Los Angeles to Washington, D.C. He was making stops along the way, and Louisville happened to be one of them. I had no idea who Arthur Blessitt was, and I can't remember what he preached. I do remember, however, the Holy Spirit moving in my life during that gathering in Freedom Hall that caused me to go down on the floor during the decision time. As I knelt, a counselor placed his hand on my back. He was gentle and kind as he asked me why I came forward. I told him I didn't know. I can't remember much of the conversation, but I remember his encouragement and at least one thing he said: "God will use you, Jimmy." God employed that moment to set me up for what would happen in four years. But first, something would happen three years later.

In 1973, during my sophomore year in high school, I was asked to serve on the pastor search committee (a.k.a. "Pulpit Committee" then) of my home church. I was one of seven persons charged with the task of finding a pastor for the church. Yes, I was the "token" young person. I didn't have much to say because, the truth is, I really didn't know what I was doing! Those six adults, though, made me feel part of that process at age 16. The chairperson in one of our meetings asked me, "Jimmy what do you expect from our next pastor?" Without hesitation I said, "I hope he can connect with young people, and I think it would be good if he were young."

The pastor we called, Bill Belva, had just graduated from the Southern Baptist Theological Seminary and was 26 years old. He was gregarious, possessed charisma, and was an excellent communicator. Like Brother Ellis, he also had an ability to see in others what they could not see in themselves. "Brother Bill" began to impact the church and community and connect with youth. He certainly impacted me.

During my high school years I worked part time as a disc jockey and news announcer for the local radio station. So, I was a celebrity of sorts (or so I thought!). Everyone knew who I was even if they didn't know me personally. My Uncle Jesse Lee was the pastor of one of the rural churches, and he invited me to speak on Youth Sunday at his church in March 1974, partly because of my "celebrity" status.

I'm embarrassed to say that I hardly prepared; I didn't take the assignment that seriously. I read some scripture and shared some of my testimony, talking for 10 or 15 minutes. During the decision time four of my peers, whom I knew on the surface but not intimately, came forward making decisions to follow Jesus for the first time or to rededicate their lives. I was dumbfounded and overwhelmed. I was also struck with fear. While I loved my Uncle Jesse Lee, I didn't feel close to him and chose not to talk to him about what happened. Instead, I talked with my pastor, Brother Bill. That's when he spoke about seeing something in me that was right for vocational ministry. I was moved to remember what that counselor said four years earlier: "God will use you, Jimmy."

I was asked to lead the congregational singing at Cadiz Baptist Church during the summer of 1974. Over the course of June and July, I was inundated with affirmation and encouragement. It was more than "You are doing a good job!" and/or "We are proud of you!" People who had watched me for nearly 18 years were seeing something in me that I knew was there. I saw it but I needed others to see it, too—and without my prompting them. All this, along with a series of small events, such as filling in for a radio preacher one morning due to his sickness, resulted in my choice to go public with my decision. Before I did, though, I spoke with my mother who had loved me unconditionally.

When I told her of my decision, she wasn't surprised. She asked me two questions: "Has God called you to do this?" and "Do you want to do this?" I responded in the affirmative to both of her questions. My mother was not an educated woman. Having been reared in abject poverty before and during the Great Depression, she completed part of the sixth grade. But she was educated. She told me that I was going to be an educated preacher because there were too many "dumb _ _ _ (first letter is A!) preachers" in our county—and that meant the entire world, too! She spoke of college and that "preacher school" (the word "seminary" wasn't in her vocabulary!) she thought was in Louisville. With her blessing I made a public commitment to enter vocational ministry on Sunday morning, August 11, 1974. It was one of the most spiritually profound moments of my life. It still is. I remember it as if it were just yesterday. I acknowledged what everyone else had seen and I had felt for a long time—more than a decade.

Over the course of the next two years—my senior year in high school and freshman year in college—I preached 51 times, supplying in churches in my home county and other locales, including Possum Kingdom, Texas. During my college freshman year another pastor, who also saw something in me, gave my name to a church looking for a summer youth minister. After interviewing with the search team, I was called to serve at Edgewood Baptist Church in Hopkinsville, Ky., for the summer of 1976 at age 19.

When I returned to Western Kentucky University in that fall to begin my sophomore year, Dr. Rollin S. Burhans, the pastor of First Baptist Church in Bowling Green, and his associate pastor, Rev. Richard W. Bridges, approached me about becoming the part-time pastor of the FBC mission church, Emmanuel Baptist Chapel. Dr. Burhans and Dick saw something in me, too. Thus, I began pastoring my first church on Monday, November 15, 1976, at age 20, and I have been a pastor ever since.

Over the course of more than four decades, since I made that public commitment in 1974, I've been the pastor of five unique congregations and am now serving my sixth pastorate. While there have been struggles and challenges, I can gladly declare that I've not regretted one moment of this life-long pilgrimage. I have also sought to see in others what they might not have seen in themselves.

"So that's how I ended up being a preacher!" And I'm not the least bit sorry that I have been and am a Christian pastor and preacher. Thanks be to God!

Jimmy Gentry is the senior pastor of Garden Lakes Baptist Church in Rome, Ga. From 1976–2016 he served as the senior pastor of five churches in Kentucky, Tennessee, and Georgia. He and his wife, Jackie, have a daughter and a son and are blessed with three granddaughters.

God's Calling to a Kid in St. Louis

Chris George

As early as I can remember, I had a strong sense of calling or, some might say, destiny. The desire was implanted in my heart. The thought dominated most of my daydreams. It was clear. I was supposed to be a professional baseball player for the St. Louis Cardinals.

Seeking to be faithful to the call, I signed up for the local little league team and religiously practiced something my dad called "the ready position." "Bend both knees, adjust your cap, put the glove on your left hand," he would tell me. This position perfectly prepares you for any ball that might be hit in your direction. I don't want to brag, but I was really good at the ready position. However, I soon learned that I was not so good at baseball. I only had about three major weaknesses: hitting, catching, and throwing, along with a slew of minor ones: running slow, lacking focus, and fearing the baseball. So, by the time I was nine years old, I had to seriously reconsider my calling.

Although I share this story in jest, I do so because my calling story started early in my life. After the dreams of being an astronaut (I hated science and got motion sickness) and a baseball player (I'm not athletic at all) died, I heard words such as minister and missionary at church. I don't think hearing those words early in life constituted a calling, but I remember that they did not scare me but seemed almost a natural fit. Perhaps it was the influence of my grandfather, Bill George, who was an honorary (meaning "unpaid") minister of music at a tiny country church in Western Kentucky, or maybe it was the stories told by the missionaries who visited our congregation.

My story never involved lightning, thunder, or a downpour of God's Holy Spirit thoroughly soaking into my soul. Instead, it felt more like dew fall. Before I realized it, I was covered with water—baptized, if you will, in calling.

As a seventh-grade student, I attended a church retreat with a clear emphasis on evangelism. We went far away from the big city of St. Louis to some forgotten corner of the world called "the Baptist Retreat Center." We didn't study the plagues that week, but we experienced the mosquitos. The stars were bright and beautiful, but the crickets were loud—not as loud, of course, as the revival preacher who talked about the importance of "getting saved" and "accepting Jesus." He concluded his remarks by saying, "If you don't know, that you know, that you know that you are saved, you better come forward and get right with the Lord."

Well, I had said the sinner's prayer, but maybe I didn't really mean it. I had been baptized, but that might have just been because of peer pressure. The more I listened to the evangelist, the more self-doubt crept in and minimized any previous religious experience. I couldn't honestly say that I knew that I knew that I knew. So, I did what I had done about 10 or 15 times before, I raised my hand and started to walk the aisle and prepared to say the sinner's prayer again.

But before I got to the front, before I met with another eager evangelist to repeat words I had said before, my youth minister redirected me to the back of the room. He whispered, "I want to talk to you." When we got to the back, he sat me down and said, "What are you doing?" I said, "Well, I was just sitting in the pew, listening and I had that sinking feeling in my stomach, and I don't know if I know if I know. So, I was just going to go ahead and walk down to the front."

He said, "I don't think you need to be saved again. I see God at work in your life. You have believed and been baptized. What are you doing?"

I said, "Well, I just felt like God was speaking to me. So, I needed to go down to the front."

Then he said words that I have never forgotten: "Chris, maybe God is speaking to you, but maybe God is not saying, 'Get saved.' Maybe God is saying something else. Instead of walking the aisle, why don't you take time to just listen tonight and we can talk tomorrow?"

It may sound silly, but it was actually an epiphany, or, really, a revelation for a kid who had grown up believing the only thing God ever said was, "Get saved." The idea that God might have a bigger vocabulary was not only earthshaking for me, but it was also life-altering.

Before bed that night I prayed, "God, I am listening . . ." Much to my disappointment, God didn't speak, at least not in an audible sort of way. I lay there and listened. The only thing I heard was the chaperone snoring.

But, looking back, God was speaking to me through a youth minister who did not talk me into walking the aisle, but rather talked me out of it. I can't tell you what happened the next day. I can't remember a single conversation, but by the time I spoke with my youth minister that night, I knew that God was calling me into ministry. I didn't know what it would look like. I didn't really need to. I was only 12. I had time.

The next Sunday I walked down the aisle of First Baptist Church of Ellisville, Mo., to respond to a calling to Christian ministry. Much to my surprise, on the same retreat two other youth from the church had experienced the same calling: another young man and a young lady (a real rarity in the Baptist churches of my childhood).

We stood before the community. There was lots of crying and hugging and hand holding. People were proud of us. God's going to do something special with you. They promised to pray for us.

What happened to the three of us?

Well, two weeks later, the young man and young lady who had stood beside me were found kissing and carousing in the church baptistery. (I don't know any of the details, but it caused quite a stir.) As far as I know, neither ever expressed any further interest in ministry. I suspect that today they are successful in other fields or vocations.

Looking back, I am just glad they were standing beside me that Sunday morning.

So, I had the odd experience of going through junior high, then high school, then college with this sense of calling. And perhaps the strangest thing of all, it did not seem unusual to me.

I didn't lead with this line when developing friendships or asking someone on a date. I don't remember engaging in many deep conversations about calling during these developmental years, but I never really doubted the validity of the calling or the course of my life.

I didn't know how I would get there, but, somehow, I knew where I was going.

The weather was not always clear. The road was often bumpy.

When my grandfather died of Lou Gehrig's disease, I was shaken and deeply disappointed with God. I was angry and felt betrayed by God, but I never even considered walking away.

When I attended Harvard Divinity School, I had a crisis of faith, but I never lost my sense of calling. In fact, ironically, it was this strong and simple calling that sustained me.

When I married a devout Catholic at St. Catherine's in New York, I wondered if there would be a place for me to serve in Baptist life.

At the time I considered these to be potential obstacles to my calling. In hindsight I see they were actually experiences that clarified my calling, which birthed within me compassion for the suffering and sorrowful, understanding for the skeptical, and appreciation for ecumenism.

Once I believed that calling came in a single moment, but now I recognize calling as a lifelong process. We come to know God, God's will, and God's way as we come to know ourselves—one conversation at a time, one situation at a time, one experience at a time.

Calling comes one day at a time, or, like the dew fall, one drop at a time.

It is past, present, and future. God called. God is calling. God will call.

And perhaps the single lesson that I learned from my short baseball career is the most important one: "The Ready Position." It takes more than a cap and a glove. It takes openness to God's Spirit and a willingness to believe that God still speaks and says more than merely, "Get saved."

Chris George is the senior pastor of Smoke Rise Baptist Church in Tucker, Ga. He previously served as the pastor of First Baptist Church of Mobile, Ala., and in ministry positions in Georgia, Kentucky, Alabama, Virginia, and Massachusetts. He and his wife, Jennifer, have four children (David, Evan, Andy, and Emma Pearl) and live in metro Atlanta.

Home Again:
A Call Narrative

Libby Grammer

Twenty-seven years ago, a strong-willed, rather precocious, six-year-old little girl decided she wanted to be like the grown-ups and get to know Jesus personally. She walked the aisle of her rural Southern Baptist church in North Georgia and prayed the sinner's prayer with her elderly pastor. A few weeks later she was baptized, and she proceeded to do everything in her power to learn about and get to know Jesus. (Whether her young mind could truly comprehend the abstract nature of God or not, her commitment was genuine.)

This little girl, the minister of music's daughter, lived at the church (almost literally for a few years, living in the pastorium next door). She loved acting in church plays, sang in children's choirs, and was watched in the pews from the choir loft by both parents every worship hour as she feigned stillness to keep up with the service. She turned pages for the pianist at hymn sings in the nursing homes, ate bounteous potluck dinners, and had more grandmothers than she could count. But, as music ministry (any ministry) often does, tastes changed, the pastor changed, and the family moved on from that rural little church home. This scenario continued again all the way out in Clovis, N.M., at a Southern Baptist church for a few years, and again, back in Georgia just north of Atlanta at yet another SBC church.

The girl grew, becoming a teenager, and though burned some by "church people" (and watching her distressed parents deal with move after move), she still found herself called to something more in her faith journey. At a Youth Evangelism Conference in the late 1990s she walked her 13-year-old self to the prayer rooms and dedicated her life to the ministry. She informed her church, and while they affirmed her calling, most in the congregation would not have approved of any work outside of perhaps missions or children's ministry (where she would not be ordained—and likely only called "director").

In middle and high school she worked with Christian groups at school in addition to her youth group: She was chaplain and president of Y-Club and led Bible studies in the morning at school. She gathered hundreds for evangelical meetings such as "See You at the Pole." She preached sermons (though she likely would not have called them that) to move her student body toward a holier way of living. Then, as it happened at age 16, moving became too much for her soul. Her youth pastor left first. Then other staff members. Her dad hung on. But then he too decided to start afresh.

Ripped from her successful high school life in her junior year, she was moved from a thriving Atlanta suburb to a small North Georgia town where her parents had grown up. The church her father moved for was in turmoil and let her father go just a year into his ministry there, and her school was less than adequate and frustratingly backward at times. Hurt one too many times by churches, angry with God for the pain she and her family endured, and with her family only attending sporadically at her mother's home church with her grandmother, she lost her interest in serving God's people.

In college she skipped Baptist Collegiate Ministries and its "church people." She continued to stay angry with God and, though trying to find a church home off and on, never felt right anywhere in Rome, Ga. She chose to major in Spanish and focus her energies on something completely different. Surely, she had heard that "call" wrong all those years ago. It wasn't worth the heartache.

Her college—Shorter College, also embroiled in the SBC turmoil—did require a couple of religion courses, though, and she of course obliged. Then, one day, she entered one of these classes with Dr. Robert Wallace. She learned to read Scripture with new eyes. She no longer felt as though Christians had to be backward and not use their brains when they sought faith. Science was no longer an obstacle to Scripture. Suddenly her faith journey was reignited. Her call was made real again in a new way. She grew in knowledge and eventually in spirit. She was still unsure about seminary and what to do next, but after many long conversations with professors, she knew she had to give it a go—and she had to do it somewhere that would fully embrace her call as a minister.

After college she was fortunate to get a job as an immigration paralegal at a local law firm just before the Great Recession hit. Just a few months into her new job she decided to apply for seminary, and she dropped to part-time work (30 hours per week) to begin attending seminary at McAfee School of Theology, a Baptist school that believed women were called to all forms of ministry. To keep a steady income, she continued to work nearly full-time hours and commuted from her home near Chattanooga to Atlanta three days a week. Despite all the busyness in her life, seminary just felt right. It allowed her to begin the journey toward a PhD in Christian ethics so that she too could provide a safe place for the questioning souls in college or seminary. She studied in the academic track and wrote a long thesis on Christian ethics and U.S. immigration (her two concurrent interests at the time).

Shortly after finishing seminary coursework, on a cold Sunday afternoon in December, she was ordained by her grandmother's little congregation in North Georgia where she had been attending during her seminary years. After her ordination she preached and led music in congregations as often as she could, but her life stayed tied up in the immigration work that paid the bills, and life happened with great force in the months after completing her seminary coursework. Shortly after her graduation her abusive, short-term marriage left her with little choice but to remove herself from the marriage and start over.

She landed in a wonderful congregation in downtown Chattanooga while living back home with her parents. Eventually she started dating and married a profoundly supportive and loving man named William. She then decided it was time to continue her pursuit of a PhD in ethics. Just six months into her new marriage she moved her new little family of two humans and two dogs to Charlottesville, Va., to complete a Master of Arts in theology, ethics, and culture at the University of Virginia as a "stepping stone" into the academy from a seminary degree. In two very harrowing and busy years she would read more theology than all three years of seminary combined, write hundreds of pages of papers including another thesis—this time on feminist theology and immigration—and complete an extremely academic degree, leaving her with little interest in continuing in the academy, at least not anytime soon. She just did not find the joy in academic life and writing that she thought she would.

She then moved to Richmond for her husband to finish his degree in mathematics at Virginia Commonwealth University, and they joined a wonderfully thoughtful and ecumenical Baptist church, River Road Church Baptist, with plenty of doctorates (both PhDs and DMins) on staff and in the congregation. She wrote a book based on her two master's theses and finally felt her academic work become more helpful to the reading public. She also began to reconsider her choice to seek a PhD and instead began contemplating church ministry for the first time in more than a decade.

To explore this further, four months into her membership at the church, she became a pastoral intern. She began to learn so much from the staff and was enjoying her work and learning opportunities when another position opened for interim minister of Christian education and spiritual formation. The church staff (and eventually the whole church) gratefully embraced her for sticking around in this new position. She held this role for more than two years, during which time she began studying for a Doctor of Ministry degree back at her home seminary, focusing on how the church might live out its ethics "on the ground." When the new pastor, Dr. Daniel Glaze, was called to RRCB, he took the time to think through how this young woman might best continue serving in ministry. Out of these conversations she then served for seven months as a pastoral resident, learning the ropes to become a senior pastor.

As part of this position, she began the sometimes-grueling waiting and interviewing process. During various interviews with churches (of which there were few looking for a young, female—and by this time, pregnant—pastor), she felt the weight of the calling taking its toll on her life. But she persevered. At first the churches didn't call back, then sometimes they would call but not follow up, until finally one day she received an email from a church in a Virginia town she'd never heard of.

Early on, she didn't know this church's rich history and its struggles and triumphs, but she would soon. Traveling three hours to the south and west of Richmond, she encountered a beautiful, small city with a large First Baptist Church, whose pastor search committee seemed excited to speak with her. Within just a couple of months she was back, visiting again, sharing her ideas and dreams for ministry with them, and listening to their history and hopes for the future. Bit by bit, the committee and she prayed, spoke, and danced with the Holy Spirit until a call weekend in June 2018 led this small congregation with a big space and big dreams to call her to a full-time senior pastorate among them.

This called, young minister and her family have been welcomed with open arms, with loving support for a family of two adult humans, now three dogs, and a new little human. The joy of everyday ministry continues in new ways as the act of preaching and leading worship every Sunday has become her own, as she visits the bereaved, as she dines with her congregants and hears their stories. This place and these people are the church universal living out the gospel story in a local context, and they are her calling.

This pastor has moved from being called to ministry to running from God to studying religion academically to attending seminary to seeking a PhD and all the way back to being called to church ministry and studying ministry deeply in a DMin program. Callings clearly are not for the faint of heart, and just like scriptural callings, often the recipients of the call are reluctant and confused, and take a winding path to answering and following. Yet, God finds ways to bless ministry when calls are eventually heeded, and this young, new mom has not only found her calling serving God's people in Martinsville, Va., but she has embraced the love and care of the church in profound new ways thanks to her experiences and growth in pastoral ministry in recent years. She may have pulled away from her calling and the church in the past, but she has now come home again.

Libby Mae Grammer is the senior pastor of First Baptist Church in Martinsville, Va. Prior to serving as a pastor, Libby worked in the field of immigration law. She lives with her husband William Underwood, her baby daughter Elena Ruth Grammer-Underwood, and three happy dogs.

Calls Come More Than Once

Elizabeth Hagan

"If you were a man, you'd make a fine preacher." These words I heard over and over again as a teen when no boys wanted to preach, and I volunteered.

The exhortation fell strangely on my ears because Southern Baptist women don't preach. They teach the women and the children. They organize the lunches. If they're really zealous, they marry missionaries and teach abroad.

So that is what I would do. I'd gravitate toward teaching. I'd study elementary education in college. I'd start thinking about living abroad.

I completed my studies with a piece of paper in my hand from Samford University that said I could be trusted with the minds of elementary and middle school kids 8–4 p.m. each day. Yet, life in my first paid post at a struggling Birmingham, Ala., school did not fit the bill.

I wanted to read and discuss books on spirituality rather than the pedagogy of 11- and 12-year-old science curriculum. I wanted to do something about the systemic problems of drug addiction, poverty, and racism. I wanted to think more about why the church sat on the sidelines allowing fixable social problems to continue—for example, the children I was teaching not receiving milk at lunchtime because of the simple and unacceptable explanation that "the cafeteria ran out."

People who knew me best then, like Renee, one of the campus ministers at Samford University, began to ask: "Have you ever considered attending seminary? I think you'd love it there."

I heard Renee out in all seriousness, because in the years during college, the classes, the people, and the travel experiences opened my mind to more than one way to live out my faith. From the church I planted myself in throughout college, it wasn't unusual for a woman to lead, attend seminary, or be unmarried well into her 30s. I saw women preach for the first time. I knew women with the "Rev" in front of their name, too. I knew how important it was to have an MDiv.

So, I began filling out my first seminary application. Even if there weren't answers for my pro-and-con checklist, it would be ok. I'd just see what happened next. The more I prayed, the more I realized I wanted to be something that did not exist.

If you asked me what this was, I'd begin to tell you that it looked something like what I saw Sarah doing—the first woman I'd ever seen serve in the "senior pastor" slot.

I'd begin to tell you that it needed to be something that excited me in the morning when I woke up and flooded my mind with ideas for when my head laid on the pillow at night.

I'd begin to tell you that this something probably had no guarantees I'd ever get a 9–5 job doing it.

I'd begin to tell you that it would have to include reading, writing, and sharing thoughts of value to me with a group of people.

And so, I whispered to a few people I trusted: "I want my work connected to the church somehow."

Joy exploded around me with the mere utterance of these few words. The more I walked toward this light of going to seminary, the brighter the confidence around me became. Yet, there were days when I lingered in the safe waters of how I might be both an elementary teacher and a pastor. I creatively stalled, saying, "Maybe I'll just work in the schools and in the church part time in the summer. Maybe I could write curriculum and be a teacher to other teachers." Of course, such a compromise would never be enough. I was born to be a pastor, and I was beginning to understand how I couldn't say no.

The first fall break home from seminary in 2003, I began to whisper: "I think I'm going to one day pastor a local church." I was confident but afraid. I knew this would change everything for me and the life everyone around me had hoped I would lead. Baptist women, I knew, just did not do such without stirring up trouble.

But those who knew me best said: "We've known this all along. Of course, you are."

Finally, I could tell the call was *happy*, but what a transition in which to live this out. The church of my childhood would not support my new intentions. My family didn't know how to support my plans. Everything felt so confusing. Would I ever be able to support myself in ministry?

Thankfully, my female seminary friends helped me to join the preacher-to-be club. We midwifed each other. Together, we cheered one another on through completion of our classes, applying for jobs, and ordination services.

From my seminary viewpoint, I believed I'd found my forever home in the local church. Throughout divinity school I heard seminary professors say that the most virtuous thing you can do for your whole life is to serve the church with an undivided heart. "The church needs you!" my classmates and I were told repeatedly. Sometimes our instructions included more details like this: "Take care of the church like nothing else matters. Live in the community where you serve, join every local board you can, and know your neighbors. Those who give their whole life to the church will not be disappointed."

One of my favorite professors at Duke Divinity School, Dr. Quick, reinforced these exhortations by continually testifying that there was nothing better he could have done in his life than to serve God's church as a preacher, teacher, caregiver, and lover of all things potluck for 40 years before coming to teach. He'd stop lectures and go into a weekly speech that honed his point: "If you are called to the church, don't stray." In the divine glow of this teacher I respected, I always nodded back in affirmation. "I won't stray," I promised him and myself too.

And, like Dr. Quick exhorted, I intentionally planted my feet in the local church.

When a Baptist church in Maryland came calling a couple months after I graduated from seminary in 2006, I said yes both to ordination and taking on a role as the church's pastor of youth and education.

When another church came calling two years later in Virginia, I said yes to "Elizabeth, senior pastor." At 28 I was both one of the youngest Baptist women in such a role and was oh so proud. I cried the entire first week of my post—tears of joy. I'd landed in the position that everyone around me said was impossible. While I knew the post came as a gift of God, I remember the words, "I did it! I did it!" coming off my lips several times. I didn't have to "start my own church" if I wanted to lead—as one denominational leader had suggested on several occasions. For that time and that place and in that season, the call was especially happy.

But I left four years later.

It wasn't that I didn't love my church (I did!). It wasn't because I lost my faith or because I got into a fight with someone on the board. It was because the call and I needed to have a chat. The call needed to tell me again who I was, even if I was slow to listen. And because of this *who* I was, I needed to take a different path.

This different path looked like pastoring by: crafting social media strategies, traveling to support my husband's work with a nonprofit, advocating for international voices to be heard as we traveled, tending to friendships with care, learning to write like a journalist, fundraising for orphans to go to college, and most of all putting words on the page—lots and lots of words on a page. Some of this I got paid for; most of it I didn't. Someone in our house needed to make a living wage: this was what mattered the most.

I began to whisper to friends in 2011, "I'm a writer . . . I think I need to write a book."

And again, they said, "We've always known."

And the call was again happy.

I published my first memoir full of words about infertility, God, and rebirth. For some, that would be enough. But the itch didn't leave. I needed to write more words—words that heal, words that connect, words that open up space for the holy to come. I'd need to learn to say I'm a writer, maybe even more than a local church pastor.

As I began to tend to this call to write, I started floating in and out of the church. I received training in interim ministry. I said yes to countless calls to supply preach and lead churches for months at a time, not years. My soul can no longer agree with the voices that say: "You should try staying put. Why can't you stay with us longer? An interim is not enough."

For in moving, I'm listening. The call smiles.

We in the church are usually about the business of saying that conversion only happens once. We take such pride in it that we write a date down and seek to treasure it forever. We pair conversion with heaven and hell and who ends up where in the end. Or in other types of churches, we might say conversion is not even how we understand faith at all. And then conversion talk stops there. Never would we pair conversion with vocation.

We teach our children: "Figure out what God wants you to do. And if you are so lucky to hear, just do it! Don't ask again." We applaud our young adults for settling into more adult ways of stable checking accounts, retirement funds, and ladder-climbing promotions. We praise our employees who have worked at the same company for 30 years.

But, as I've followed the call, I've learned that vocation has everything to do with conversion. Vocation is much more static than our best graduation speeches lead our youth to believe. The call has converted me to new "seeings" of myself that I, at first, never believed. Maybe this is not how the call beckons everyone, but it's how it's beckoned me. One of my favorite hymns has everything to do with conversion. In fact, when I married my husband, I walked down the aisle to this very tune. "He leadeth me, he leadeth me, by his own hand he leadeth me; his faithful follower I would be, for by his hand he leadeth me."

What my next phase of ministry will hold, I'm unsure. Will I still be a pastor? Will I write a lot more? Or will I do something altogether different? I don't know. And it's ok. Well, I guess, it's mostly ok (not knowing is scary stuff). All the call asks of me is that I listen, because the promise resounds loudly: God leadeth me.

Elizabeth Hagan is senior minister of the Palisades Community Church in Washington, D.C. She is the author of books such as Birthed: Finding Grace Through Infertility *(2016) and is the executive director of Our Courageous Kids, a foundation dedicated to orphan care. She's the proud mom of Amelia and wife of Kevin, with whom she's always planning their next international adventure.*

Called Because
I Could Not Sing

Dock Hollingsworth

"Let's get Dock to do a devotional." Yep, my call story started because I can't sing.

I was part of a small youth group at the First Baptist Church of Doraville, Georgia. It was in the era of Sunday night church, and my youth group put together a small vocal ensemble—six voices, I think—and the group performed at other Baptist churches on Sunday nights. My sister, my girlfriend, and some of my best buddies memorized the words to about 10 songs, wore ugly ecru dresses or the matching tie, and traveled around Atlanta. My youth minister, Bert Ross, in pity for the most musically challenged youth, said, "Let's get Dock to do a devotional." The group agreed. On a long series of Sunday nights, Morning Mist performed, and I closed out the service with a heartfelt and poorly written devotional—the exact same words every night. It was bad, but still, I was affirmed by people I admired for having some gifts for public speaking.

During my senior year of high school, I began fielding the ever-present conversation starter, "So Dock, where are you going to college and what are you planning to major in?" Based solely on a great youth group experience and the adult affirmation of my six-minute devotional, I announced that I wanted to pursue vocational ministry. The crowds cheered! All of the important adults in my life celebrated and affirmed me. One Sunday I went down front at the First Baptist Church and told my pastor, Bill Doverspike, that I was surrendering to full-time Christian ministry. That is what we said back then: I was never under assault and was getting all kinds of support for my noble vocational choice, but for some reason I was told that I was "surrendering" to the ministry.

I asked my Episcopalian high school counselor, Charles Gardner, about college choices. He said, "If I were a Baptist and preparing for ministry, I'd go to Mercer University in Macon." I had never heard of Mercer, but his endorsement was enough. I told my parents about my college hopes, and they gulped hard since private school tuition was not in the plans. As a gift of God's providence, my mother took a job on the Mercer/Atlanta campus that allowed me to attend the university in Macon tuition-free.

The First Baptist Church of Doraville was a warm, affirming, blue-collar church populated mostly by employees of the nearby General Motors plant. That congregation loved me and nurtured my calling. I preached on Youth Sunday and even filled the pulpit on a few Sunday nights. I shudder to think what I inflicted on those saints; still, they loved me and encouraged me. But First Baptist's best gift to me was an introduction to Melissa Brown. She was stunning and out of my league, even when wearing the Morning Mist, ecru polyester dress. We began dating in the spring of my senior year of high school. When I went to Mercer, Melissa was still in Atlanta. Our long-distance courtship involved several conversations about what a life of shared ministry might look like. To my great delight, she was ready to take the journey with me, and we've been ministering together ever since.

In the year since I had declared my call to vocational ministry, and before beginning Mercer, my call story was smooth and encouraging, the stuff of a Hallmark After School Special. But my first year at Mercer was when the vocational crisis hit. Like every ministerial student, I immediately got involved in the Baptist Student Union (BSU). I was also part of a subgroup of the BSU, the Ministerial Association. Believe it or not, there were enough of us preparing for vocational ministry that we had a robust club with programs and speakers. My freshman year I also pledged the Sigma Nu Fraternity.

The tension between my involvement in BSU and the fraternity was the spark that ignited my crises of vocation. I loved hanging out with my fraternity friends; my best friends at school were part of Sigma Nu. We played intramural sports together; ordered late-night Domino's Pizza; and talked honestly about girls, upcoming exams, and life choices. Fraternity friends affirmed my calling and later voted for me to serve as Sigma Nu chaplain.

On the other hand, the Ministerial Association was not nearly as welcoming. They challenged my participation in a social fraternity. One officer of the group, whom I barely knew, confronted me at a meeting and said, "You know that part of your dues goes to buy beer, don't you?" The guys in the Ministerial Association (yes, in those days it was all guys) seemed pious and plastic in ways that I was not, and I could not see becoming like them. They brought briefcases to class, carried Bibles to Algebra, and distanced themselves from the rest of college life. My broader college involvements made me suspect to them, and I was never fully part of their group.

Not fitting in with the other ministerial students caused me to doubt my calling. I assumed that a call to ministry meant a call to be one of them. I assumed that I had misunderstood what I thought to be God's call on my life. I thought my only options were to become like the others preparing for ministry or to change my vocational course. I struggled. I prayed. I howled at the moon. I walked the campus with friends and talked and anguished. "Everybody at home, at church—they are going to be disappointed in me," I thought. I anguished some more. Finally, I realized that I just could not ever see myself as an honest part of the Ministerial Association: it was time to give up on ministry.

I made an appointment to go see my academic advisor, Dr. Howard Giddens. He had been the pastor of First Baptist Church in Athens, Ga., for 18 years before teaching Old Testament at Mercer. My very first college course, at 8:00 Monday morning, was Introduction to Old Testament with Howard Giddens, and I liked and trusted him. The afternoon of my appointment, I walked down a quiet linoleum hallway to his office in Knight Hall. I was there simply to tell my advisor that I wanted to change my major and to complete the needed paperwork, but as I began explaining, I started to cry.

Embarrassed by my emotion, I started slobbering and blurting incomplete sentences about how I didn't want to be a pastor, how I couldn't be all plastic and phony, how I wasn't going to turn my back on my fraternity friends, how I just couldn't be as pious as a minister had to be. When I finished my tirade, Dr. Giddens spoke slowly, "Boy, there's hope for you. The only way to make it in ministry is for a real calling to get integrated with a real life. Nobody can fake it for the long haul. All the good ones have struggled with this integration. I am not going to give you the forms to change your major today. Instead, I want you to meet with me for the next several weeks at this time, and let's talk. If my instincts are right, you are just beginning to do the hard work that all the good ones must do." Howard Giddens saved me.

I never did change my Christianity major. (Since I knew my roommate's student number, I did, however, find the forms and I declared a new major for him. I think Jeff Porter spent a year as a Women and Gender Studies major before he found out. Clearly, God had more work to do in my life.) Instead of changing my major, I enrolled in all of the Bible and ministry classes I could get my hands on. I loved what I was studying, and I trusted and even embraced the struggle of trying to figure out how a holy God could endorse and shape a guy like me for ministry.

I graduated with my Christianity major in June of 1984. Melissa and I got married in our church in Doraville in July, and we loaded my lime green 1972 Ford Pinto and moved to seminary in August. While a student at Southeastern Baptist Theological Seminary, my calling deepened. I found ministerial students whom I liked and admired. I found professors who challenged my narrow, but sure, thinking. I found new gifts for ministry and continued affirmation that I was unpacking an authentic call to serve God's church.

While I was a student I served the Warrenton Baptist Church in Warrenton, N.C., as the "Minister of Everything Else." The pastor, Ed Beddingfield, and I were the only two staff members, and I was part time. But this loving community let me try my hand at leadership and loving and planning trips and ordering curriculum and spaghetti supper fundraisers. I loved my youth group and went to their ballgames and graduations, and they let me into their lives.

Ed was a pipe-smoking, Yale Divinity graduate with a beard and a Volvo. I had never met a pastor like Ed. And I watched him preach and love and serve with effective delight. As the church followed Ed's love for them and gave me space to fumble and try, I began to claim that God really could call and shape a variety of people into effective ministry. If God could use this New Haven liberal this effectively, maybe I had a chance!

The Warrenton Baptist Church initiated my ordination process, and I called Bill Doverspike back in Doraville and asked him if he would lead the process and let me come home and be ordained by the church that first saw some glimmer of God's call on my life. The certificate hangs on my office wall, with 12 now-faded signatures. I look back at it from time to time with gratitude for the risk they took and for the churches that made my formation part of their mission.

I suppose if I had been able to sing, I might have been given an ecru, polyester tie and this story would have turned out differently. But I am grateful for the turns that led me down the path of ministry. I am grateful for God's tenacious providence—*still* trying to shape me into the minister I was called to be. And I am grateful for the churches and individuals who loved me into this amazing work for the Kingdom of God.

Dock Hollingsworth is senior pastor of Second-Ponce de Leon Baptist Church in Atlanta, Ga., following an 18-year career at the James and Carolyn McAfee School of Theology at Mercer University. Dock is still married to the girl in the ecru dress. He and Melissa have adult twins and love having grandchildren nearby.

Not Me? Yes, You!

Les Hollon

I am a pastor. There I said it. Here I write it. My identity didn't come easily. I did not want to be a pastor. Christian? Yes! Preacher? Gladly. But not a pastor.

Who wants to be controlled by the whims of people who have the power to openly criticize you and your family for running up the electricity bill by using the parsonage air conditioner 24/7 during the hot days of a Texas summer? Not me. Who wants to get publicly slapped on the wrist for not buying the meat for fellowship meals on sale at the Riverside Market? Not me.

I heard plenty of this small-minded thinking as a boy while sitting next to my mother during too many Baptist business meetings. She was the church clerk. She was courageous. She spoke with tough character and a tender heart to people who became Baptist bullies at business meetings. But they kept on. It all led to the infamous "called meeting." There people turned their fussing into feuding, wanting our pastor, Bro. Mac, to leave. The feuders didn't have the votes, but they had the power to break his and his family's heart . . . mine too. He left. I didn't. My response was to resist any urging to become the pastor of a local church.

So I preached, I led, I served, I "faithed" all during high school and into college. The second time I preached, the worship service kept going. It wasn't my sermon that wouldn't stop; it was the singing.

I was 15, preaching the Sunday evening service of a weekend revival. My brother and a friend of his from Baylor University preached the earlier services. Hearts were touched. People were helped. The gospel went forward.

No one was expecting what ended up happening that last night. We sang. We prayed. People testified. What my sermon lacked in content, which was much, was made up by my enthusiasm.

For revivals, the invitation is the high moment of worship. That's an evangelical term for when people update their relationship with God: accept Jesus, confess sin, join the church, rededicate one's life to the Christian way, or any other response that draws people closer to God.

That night the Spirit was free to move; and move she did. Our invitation hymn was the classic, "Just As I Am," made famous by the Billy Graham crusades. We started to sing, and people started to come. They came forward for an hour. We sang all six verses so many times that those who already didn't have it memorized had it down pat before the last amen was spoken. We caught the cadence of "Just as I am without one plea . . . I come! I come! Just as I am and waiting not to rid my soul of one dark blot . . ."

Many who came forward were my classmates. Some had participated with me since the seventh grade in a weekly prayer-and-share time. We would meet in different homes throughout the year to talk about things spiritual, look at Scripture, pray, laugh, and occasionally cry together. On that night the Spirit moved to help us claim a common identity in Christ. Others also came who were younger and older than I. We knew that we needed something more in our lives, and Christ was our bridge into the future. God's grace held us close.

It was a few years later that God did what God does. He called me to trust him with the very calling I did not want. It happened during my sophomore year at Baylor. I was minding my own business while worshiping during a Sunday evening musical drama worship service at my college church, Columbus Avenue Baptist. The musical was audaciously titled, *The Call*.

The problem was that God was not minding his business. He started meddling in mine. I became angry and walked out during the invitation. You know that time in a Baptist service when you are asked to walk the aisle by going forward not backwards?!

Well, I walked out. I was saying to myself that this was a poorly conducted service—shallow lyrics, out-of-tune instrumentalists, and off-key singers. Other than that, I guess it was okay but not for me. All of a sudden, this small-town boy had become an urbane music critic.

When I walked out the entry door, I stopped in my tracks underneath the massive Grecian columns that graced the church building's portico and asked myself why I was so angry. Then God's call called out: "Trust me. Just trust me." So instead of leaving, I walked back inside and down that same aisle I had used as my exit. Then and there, I confessed to my college minister and the church that God was calling me to be, of all things, a pastor.

I still resisted. Trust comes hard to a broken heart. I thought if the pastorate worked out like I feared, then I would leave seminary, go to law school, and become an attorney and a politician. I was upfront about my resistance. I wrote it into my application. They took me seriously. The admissions office gave me provisional acceptance and placed me on probation. My sense of call was to be reviewed after my first semester.

I later became the pastor of the professor who interviewed me to remove my probationary status. We chuckled about it. I chuckled again last August when officiating the graveside service for a former Texas governor. There at the state cemetery in Austin, speaking the gospel into the hearts of our state's leading politicians, I realized once again how good it was to be standing in my calling and not in theirs.

God's humor struck my funny bone. I am still laughing at the irony of my calling, all these years later. Not me? Yes me!

Nine years ago the Spirit whispered to me yet again: "Trust me. I am calling you to Trinity. And I will *prune* you." I had never warmed up to the feeling of being *pruned*. Pain, not pleasure, seemed to control the pruning metaphor of John 15:2. But because it was a Jesus-teaching, I knew it was rooted in a reality I could not afford to ignore. So, I said yes to Trinity and to the pruning by moving from Louisville, Ky., to San Antonio, Texas.

This is a good calling, and I've come to peace with the pruning. Because along the way I've understood why the two are inseparable. Pruning is the ongoing work of being a called leader. In this fast-paced and ever-changing world, a leader, particularly a pastor, must be shaped by the one who is the alpha and omega of time, and who is the author and finisher of our faith. We must grow to help others grow.

This is why Jesus included the second half of the John 15:2 dictum. He prunes the branch so that it will be even more fruitful. Producing more of God's promise in our world and in people means that more and more of God must be at work in the leader. Our ego must be pruned. Our false sense of self must be uprooted. Our ego must be made strong and healthy by the awareness that life includes us but is not just about us. Our calling as a servant leader enables us to envision God's hope without it being centered around our ego comforts.

God's call touches the heart, engages the head, and empowers the hand. God's pruning ways continue to shape our call by:

LISTENING through prayer. Sometimes I'll pray for minutes on end without any sense of connecting to God. Then the Spirit seems to prune with, "Okay, now that you've prayed out your agenda, are you ready just to be with me and to listen to me?" The early Christians called this *kenosis*, the emptying of oneself before God. This detaches us from our personal agendas and needs long enough for them to be purified and refined by spiritual examination.

TALKING with and not just "at" people. Hear what they are saying and not saying. As Lyndon B. Johnson observed, people are always sending messages to leaders. Receive affirmation and criticism with equal humility. The good is not to puff up the ego but to encourage you—to stay true to God's call. The criticism is food for thought—to grow and strengthen God's call. Eat your vegetables. Stand in the shoes of the critics to grasp the truth of their message and to let go of the sting. Be pruned by applying the truth and discarding the "noise."

CREATING Q&A sessions. At the end of your presentation in meetings, don't walk away until you've asked for responses. Your willingness conveys transparency that in turn builds trust. Some people will sharpen your perspective and be a needed reality check. Others will feel heard and therefore included. Those bent on just being "troublemakers" will expose themselves. Be pruned by conversation.

MEDITATING on Scripture. The Apostle Paul's admonition to Timothy connects us to a practice we all need: seeing that Scripture is God's inspired pruning message for "profit, correction, and instruction in righteousness" (2 Tim. 3:16). Spend time in the Word so your words will be worthy.

SMILING when you hear your predecessor's name. My three predecessors at Trinity Baptist Church were strong personalities and very gifted. Be encouraged that you are included in the conversation. Don't build yourself up by tearing down those who worked before you. Be pruned by letting others be praised. Celebrate in the part of their work that still helps the church today. Even when you know the "inside story," don't step into the counterproductive trap of defensiveness. Don't get distracted. Move the conversation forward. And remember that one day you will be a "predecessor."

FEELING the needs of people. Be available. Ultimately, leadership and ministry are about relationships, engaging in the sacredness of God's hope for humanity. Before and after gatherings, be available for people to connect with you. Let them know how they can reach you. Go where they are. Visit in their homes, workplaces, or over coffee, or by text, phone, and email. We must prune our schedules for solitude and community. By crying and laughing with people, we are pruned by the hurts and hopes of people.

STUDYING best practices and discerning transferable principles. Continuous research and development position us to build on the best of what we know by learning what we need to know but don't yet comprehend. Be pruned of ignorance. We live in a learning culture. Let a child teach you technology. Let an older person teach you wisdom. Read to learn. Listen to podcasts for growth. Ask your peers how they do what they do. Lean into the gifts of people to make the church whole. Be the best version of yourself by learning from the best of others.

MENTORING the next generation. Be pruned of feeling irreplaceable. Remember that life includes you but is not just about you. Be a giver to the future. Build your legacy one day at a time by daily investing in others. Help others to surpass you. Be smart about it. Don't give away what is yours to do from the uniqueness of who you are, but don't cling to opportunities that are to be shared with others so they can thrive and the gospel can win. We must see beyond ourselves if we are to help others see their abilities and find their place. Share. Be generous.

Pruning is yielding to God's best so we can be our best. The pain is temporary. The pleasure is eternal. Accept God's invitation to John 15:2 leadership. Trust God to prune you.

Les Hollon is a family man, pastor, preacher, professor, and writer. He loves people and enjoys laughing, hiking, and traveling. He is the senior pastor of Trinity Baptist Church in San Antonio, Texas. His wife Vicki is also a vocational minister, and together they have served in various global regions.

An Unforgettable Calling

Barry Howard

Mrs. Gibson, my fourth-grade teacher, asked our class to write about "What I Want to Be When I Grow Up." She was the first, but certainly not the last, to inquire about our childhood vocational dreams.

When *Apollo 11* landed on the moon on July 20, 1969, I was staying at the home of my aunt and uncle in Athens, Ala. My uncle worked at the Redstone Arsenal in Huntsville, so the lunar landing was a big deal. As I watched the televised touchdown, I decided right then and there that I wanted to be an astronaut.

That is, until 1972 when Clyde Bolton, a classmate of my father, published his book *The Crimson Tide: A Story of Alabama Football.* After devouring the book, my vocational aspirations changed: I wanted to be a football coach. A year later, as a seventh grader, I took my first agriculture class and subsequently joined the Future Farmers of America. After attending the state FFA convention in Montgomery, I decided that I wanted to become an agronomist.

But there comes a time when vocational dreams and aspirations give way to an inner sense of calling, a response to deeply spiritual and internal conversation that is difficult to explain. For some, it emerges early in life. For others, it comes later.

For me, that profound and durable sense of calling came early. During the latter part of my sophomore year in high school, for some unexplained reason I started listening more intently to my pastor's sermons. I was not only inspired by the content but also began to notice his mannerisms, to anticipate his illustrations, to marvel at his ability to speak without looking at his notes, and to say to myself, "I don't think I could ever be a pastor."

No one ever said to me, "I think you should become a pastor." However, for a couple of Sundays, when I sat in church listening to our pastor, I began to imagine myself in the pulpit preaching. I would quickly block out that visual image, because the last thing I wanted to do as an introverted teenager was to stand up in front of people and speak.

The next week, as I was mowing my grandparents' lawn, I found myself preaching a sermon in my head. I was so bothered by this mental wandering that I lost my appetite and an internal argument began, almost like I was wrestling with God. The more I tried to envision myself in the agribusiness field calibrating grain drills or projecting crop production, the more my mind turned to planting seeds through preaching.

I had always looked forward to going to church, but as Sunday approached, my inner turmoil became more chaotic. I didn't want to think about going to church. I didn't want to tell anyone about my spiritual wrestling match. I didn't want to hear anyone say, "You're only 16 and far too young to know what you are 'called to do' with your life."

However, skipping church was not an option in our family at that point. On Sunday morning I found myself preaching the sermon in my head, even as my pastor preached the sermon from the pulpit. I was relieved when the service was finally over.

In those days we went to church on Sunday morning and evening. As we prepared for the evening service to begin, I felt conflicted. I certainly wanted to be obedient to the leadership of the Spirit, but I preferred a quiet obedience—not a vocation of being in front of hundreds of people every week.

As the service progressed and the sermon began, for the first time I can recall, I tried to tune out the pastor. I didn't want to come to terms with this sense of conscription welling up within me. But then a mysterious thing happened. Our pastor, Rev. Tommy Reaves ("Brother Tommy"), stopped in the middle of the sermon and simply said, "I think someone here is being called to preach tonight, so I think we'll just stop and sing the invitation hymn." That event and those words both scared me and confirmed what was taking place inside of me.

Earlier, at age 14, when I made my public profession of faith, I had gone to speak to the pastor privately. I did not "walk the aisle" in the traditional sense. First, I didn't want to walk in front of the congregation with all eyes focused on me. And second, I had experienced multiple public invitations that were emotionally manipulative.

But on this memorable evening in May of 1976, I spontaneously shed all apprehension and quickly "walked the aisle" and said to Brother Tommy, "I think it's me." And I remember him saying, "I think it's you, too."

I've thought a lot through the years about that unusual call experience. In my 40 years of ministry I have observed the Spirit's leadership regularly, but I never heard or desired to hear the audible voice of God. Yet, I must confess that I never heard the voice of God as loudly as I did when I experienced the confirmation of my calling as a 16-year-old.

I'm not sure why my call was so emphatic, unless God knew that with my tendency toward self-doubt that I needed a landmark moment to punctuate the authenticity of my calling.

In the days following that Sunday evening announcement, I met with Brother Tommy regularly. First, he explained that a call to ministry could be a call to many things. Some are called to be pastors, some missionaries, some evangelists, some writers, and some teachers or professors. He encouraged me to pray that God would clarify my call in the years ahead. Second, he encouraged me to prepare for college. Only two people in our congregation had ever been to college, and no one in my immediate family had ever finished high school. So, going to college had previously seemed beyond the realm of possibility.

During these early days, over and over again, Brother Tommy affirmed God's call on my life. In later years, when I became a pastor, I tried to always affirm the young men and women in my purview who sensed God's call to ministry.

Looking back, that early encouragement from my pastor gave me the courage to stand in front of people with confidence, because I knew the Lord was with me, and I knew my pastor had my back. Brother Tommy had such confidence in my call that he asked me to preach my first sermon on June 5. Then he recommended that I volunteer at a Bible camp near Rome, Ga., where the leaders quickly made me one of the camp pastors. Yes, as a naïve but passionate 16-year-old, I preached at Peach State Bible Camp for eight weeks in the summer of 1976. When I returned home from camp, Brother Tommy called his friends to let them know of this "preacher boy" who would make a good speaker for their Youth Day or Student Sunday.

I've never forgotten my pastor's encouragement or his networking skills. To this day, 42 years later, he is still one of the most important people in my life. Thanks to the domino effect of his early contacts, I had preached in 38 of the 67 churches in our local Baptist association by the time I graduated from high school.

At that time, Brother Tommy had a high school education and a few courses in business that had equipped him for his career in the grocery industry. Although he had been a bi-vocational pastor early in his ministry, he served as a full-time pastor at our church. In retrospect, I learned that he created for me opportunities he had not been afforded to continue his education.

Thanks to many encouragers, I not only graduated from high school, but also finished near the top of my class. I completed my bachelor's degree at Jacksonville State in Alabama, graduating with honors in 1983. I was privileged to study at New Orleans Baptist Theological Seminary, primarily at the Birmingham campus, and completed my Master of Divinity degree in 1991. And shortly after I finished my degree, Brother Tommy, who had moved to Georgia by then, enrolled in the Atlanta campus of New Orleans Theological Seminary, and his dream of completing his theological education became a reality.

My trek may seem unusual now. Most students complete their education and then begin serving. However, I was called to serve as an associate minister just after high school, and then became a full-time pastor between my sophomore and junior years in college. The experience of serving a church while attending college and seminary was a vital part of my education. Theological education for me was more practicum than theory. Looking back, my first few years of service were like a ministerial residency, and several local pastors became my coaches.

When I transitioned from serving as an associate pastor to becoming a full-time pastor, I was quite anxious about the task of preaching every week on Sunday morning, Sunday evening, and Wednesday night. Roughly, that amounted to about 144 preparations per year when I factored in two weeks of vacation and special events. Brother Tommy underscored for me that "people will forgive a lot of bad preaching if you know their name and they know you care for them." I found that to be true throughout my ministry.

My first pastorate was at the Post Oak Springs Baptist Church near Jacksonville, Ala. This courageous church had the audacity to call a 22-year-old, single college student as its interim pastor, then a few months later as pastor.

Little did I know that my call to Post Oak would ignite a minor controversy in the local association. My age wasn't an issue, but my bachelor status was. Some of the brethren held to a strict interpretation that the phrase from 1 Timothy 3 about being "the husband of one wife" required that a pastor have not more than one, and not less than one. The congregation quickly set to remedy the situation by suggesting various candidates to be my wife, overtures that I diplomatically deflected.

After serving the church for two years, I did quietly begin dating the church pianist who was completing her freshman year at Jacksonville State. On January 15, 1985, I proposed to Amanda Marie Nance, and we were married later that year on September 7. Interestingly, Amanda felt "called" to be a pastor's wife. And in most of our places of service, I think the church at times tolerated me in order to hang on to her.

We have been blessed to serve in churches that have appreciated our gifts and respected our limitations. Looking back, I have very few regrets. I loved serving as a pastor. I treasured the opportunity to cultivate a "healthy family system" in the congregations I served. And I am grateful for the opportunity to be with people in all seasons of life.

To be honest, there were a few occasions where I was tempted to leave ministry, a dilemma almost every pastor faces at some point in his or her ministry. Sometimes the temptation to exit ministry was due to fatigue and other times due to my frustration with the messiness of congregational life. But that unforgettable memory of my call to ministry reminded me that the God who called me was the God who would also help me to navigate even the more turbulent experiences in church life.

In 2018, after serving for 39 years in pastoral ministry, I felt the call to transition from serving as a senior pastor to nurturing healthy practices among clergy and congregations.

A call to ministry is a lifetime calling, but the pastoral calling may have many different seasons and diverse expressions. I loved being the pastor of a local congregation. And now I love serving as a short-term pastor to transitioning congregations and, in small ways, as a pastor to pastors.

Despite the occasional hurdles and what the Apostle Paul referred to as "the daily burden" of the church (2 Cor. 11:28), I am grateful for my calling. For me, pastoral ministry is an engaging and meaningful vocation.

Barry Howard served as the senior minister of the First Baptist Church of Pensacola, Fla., from 2005–2017. Previously he was the pastor of churches in Alabama and Kentucky. He currently serves as a coach, consultant, and columnist with the Center for Healthy Churches. Barry and his wife, Amanda, live on the beautiful emerald coast of Florida.

Is This the Call of God?

David W. Hull

My father was a Baptist minister. As I was growing up, he served as a professor and administrator in a seminary and later as the pastor of a church. He often traveled on weekends to preach and teach in churches all around the country. Most of our family vacations were related to some speaking engagement. I watched my teacher/administrator/ preacher/pastor dad as he did his work. Early on in life, I knew what I wanted to be when I grew up. I was going to be a lawyer!

I had nothing against the ministry as a vocational calling, but I figured that was what my dad did, and I was going to do something else. Perhaps I was influenced by lawyer television shows such as *Perry Mason* in making my decision. Or, my decision may have come from the fact that most of my friends who had lawyer dads lived in bigger houses than we did. I was locked in on this vocational career path. In junior high I participated in the Optimist Oratorical Contest. In one pre-contest interview, I was asked how I planned to use this experience with public speaking when I grew up. With great clarity and certainty, I explained how this contest was preparing me for speaking in the courtroom as a lawyer. Little did I know that this preparation was for another journey.

Vanderbilt University became my college because of its great law school, and I figured that a degree from there would help me to get in a law school wherever I wanted to go. Entering as a freshman, my vocational path was very clear. "I am pre-law," I would say when asked what I was studying. As a very young boy, I probably said that I wanted to be a fireman or something like that. Later, I am sure that I wanted to be an NBA star. But, realistically, the only career I ever thought about and talked about was law. In college I worked in a law firm just to get a little experience. I was well on my way to becoming an attorney.

College has a way of helping you sort through your priorities. Along the way, maybe around my junior year, I began to wonder if law was the path for me. After all, I would have to go to three more years of school after college. I was not sure I wanted that. And, what if I was not accepted by the school I wanted? My active involvement in fraternity life had kept me from being the scholar I could have been. Would my average grades get me into the competitive world of law school? I didn't think they would, so I changed direction. I would become a tycoon instead of a lawyer! Business administration became my major, and I was set free to think of getting a good job in the business world after graduation without needing any more school. My label changed from "I am in pre-law" to "I am in business." I was on my way to the land of prosperity.

Then it happened. The summer before my senior year in college I was dating a young woman in the church where my dad was the pastor. One night she and I were sitting in my car talking in front of her house, and she wanted to share a "deep, dark secret" with me. For a split-second, I wondered what she could possibly say to me that was such a secret. Then she said, "I feel that God is calling me to be a missionary." Wow. I had known many missionaries through the years, but most of them were older women with buns on the top of their heads! (Not really, but that was my stereotype.) Now, this cute, blond sorority girl was talking about a mysterious calling from God to become a missionary. I was stunned. We talked more that night. I listened to her passion, excitement, and dreams about this possible calling. I went home and slept restlessly.

The next morning was a holiday, the bicentennial of our country: July 4, 1976. Lying in bed that morning, the thought hit me for the first time in my life: "If God could use a girl like her, could God use a guy like me?" I'd never thought seriously about ministry as a vocation for myself. I did not have to go to work that morning in the accounting firm that was preparing me for my business career, so I walked down the hallway in my home to my dad's empty study and pulled a book from the shelf. I had heard my childhood pastor, John Claypool, often mention some preacher named Harry Emerson Fosdick from the great Riverside Church in New York City. I came across a book titled *Riverside Sermons* by Fosdick. I took this book off the shelf and back to my bedroom, where I began to read, wonder, think, and pray.

The thoughts raced back and forth in my head. On one hand, I was wondering, "Is this the call of God into the vocational ministry?" I had been around churches enough that I was aware of such a call. Dad had taken a similar U-turn during college and changed from a pre-med path at one university to major in religion at a different school in response to this mysterious call from God. The language and concept of this call were not foreign to me; I had just never thought it would happen to me. On the other hand, doubts haunted me. I quickly reasoned that this was not the call of God: it was merely an attraction to the woman I was dating. On top of that, I was almost finished with my studies that had prepared me for one vocational path. Interviews for management jobs in the business world would begin in the fall semester when I returned to school. This was no time to change horses in the middle of the stream.

Like Jacob by the Jabbok River, I wrestled silently with these thoughts for days, and then months. I went back to college and continued to wrestle. I confided in no more than five people this crazy idea that was taking up residence in my mind and heart. I did not have a faith community at school that would give me a safe place to talk through this call. A few friends and I attended worship in churches with some regularity, but I did not know anyone in the church. I had stepped foot in the Baptist Student Union one time, and that was to play ping pong. My community was my fraternity, and these guys were not the ones to help me discern the call of God. I was their president at the time and outwardly continued to pursue the vocational path I had chosen, while in my heart I was struggling and torn with uncertainty about my future. It only grew worse with every job interview I had.

The Thanksgiving holiday arrived, and I returned home for the first time in the semester. I still had not told my parents anything about this. Now was the time to have a talk. My dad and I sat in my parents' bedroom and I said, "Dad, you may not believe this, but I think God is calling me into the ministry." He smiled and said, "Mom and I have known this all along. We wondered how long it would take you to sense the call. God has given you gifts and experiences that have prepared you to be a wonderful minister." I was stunned. "You knew all along! Why have you not said anything to me about it?" He replied, "We have never mentioned this to you. The call must come from God. We have seen too many children of ministers who seemed to be called by Mom or Dad instead of by God. We waited for you to sense the call from God." I have always felt blessed by my parents, but never more than that moment. It was the gift of blessing I needed.

But I still was not exactly sure. Job interviews were going well. Over the Christmas break I returned to my hometown for a second interview with a bank. All day I met people in the bank and at the end of the day I was offered a job. There it was: everything I had worked for during four years of college. Back in the city I loved, a job in the business world was waiting for me. This could be the first of many steps to becoming the president of a bank. "I can't do it," I said. "I cannot accept your offer. You see, I now know that I am being called into the ministry. I plan to return to this same city and attend seminary." I am sure that bank's vice president had never heard that before from a candidate, and he probably cursed me after I left for wasting his day. It turns out, he was the first person I told about my decision to follow the call of God into ministry. It's strange, really. I guess I needed to walk right up to the brink of my own vocational dreams before I could say yes to the only path that was right for me.

Looking back now after 40 years of pastoral ministry, I can see how God was preparing me for a life of service in the church. Those public speaking contests prepared me for something much better than the courtroom, the business courses gave me an understanding of how organizations work, and the leadership experiences equipped me for the challenging role of pastoral leadership. Without my awareness, my call was happening over the course of many years. Then there were those critical moments that shape a lifetime. To use the language of biblical calls, there was my "burning bush" that came through the voice of a young woman, a profound "blessing" that came through my dad, months of "wrestling" with the call, occasional conversations with trusted friends, and finally a moment of decision in a bank building that radically changed the trajectory of my life.

I do not say that I "surrendered to the call." While that language is often used, I have chosen to say that I "accepted the call." After all, this call to vocational ministry is all grace. I did nothing to make it happen. On my own, I would have gone a different direction. But when the gift appeared in a way that I could understand, I accepted the calling as a gift. What a gift it has been!

David Hull served as the pastor of the First Baptist churches in Laurens, S.C.; Knoxville, Tenn.; and Huntsville, Ala. Currently he is the associate pastor of Second-Ponce de Leon Baptist Church in Atlanta and a consultant with the Center for Healthy Churches.

When God Surprised Me

Jane Hull

Call: It is an interesting word that, in and of itself, conjures up many different meanings. I truly believe we are all called, laity and clergy alike, and my story encompasses both categories. My own call to ministry is extraordinarily unique because I experienced it at two different times, during two different ministry life stages, in two very different ways.

Do you remember how and when you first came to faith? For some people it is immediate, instantaneous. A person may be a teenager at camp during an altar call, in the crowd at a revival meeting, or simply listening for God's voice, and suddenly a "lightning bolt" goes off and she finds herself on her knees before God. Because of the similarity with the biblical story of Saul's conversion experience in Acts 9, this type of response is often called a "Damascus Road" experience—a profound life-changing event that turns a person from unbelief into a follower of Jesus.

A call to ministry can occur in a similar fashion. A person might be a new believer or a long-time disciple of Jesus, when, suddenly, a call to ministry comes to him. It could happen in much the same way as a call to faith—immediate or instantaneous. Perhaps he is sitting in silence, hearing words from a preacher, or in a classroom, and in that setting he suddenly hears the voice of God calling him into ministry—a call that is life-changing.

There is another way to come to both faith and vocational ministry. Instead of a one-time event where someone can name the specific time and place, that Damascus Road experience, the call might be the result of years of listening for God's voice or learning from teachers and pastors who have gently provided guidance and mentoring.

I am sharing these possibilities because my own calling encompasses two different parts—a beautiful juxtaposition of both a call that developed over many years and a call that came in an immediate way. Here is my story.

I grew up in a Christian home—your typical 60s family—where we were at church every time the door was open: Sunday morning, Sunday night, Wednesday night, and other days as needed. I participated in GAs, children's and youth choirs, Sunday School, youth group, youth camps, retreats, mission trips, and the list could go on and on. In addition to my home church, I was part of a Pioneer Girls organization at another church and also strongly invested in Young Life. As a third grader, I memorized 300 Bible verses through Children's Bible Mission, which awarded me a free week at Bible camp for my efforts. I continued to return, year after year, as a camper, and later as a counselor during my college days.

Throughout these early years of my life I found myself fully immersed in these faith experiences, so it was not a stretch for me to become a believer and be baptized at an early age. My faith grew through consistent, faithful teachers and ministers, my parents, and my friends. For me, there was no sudden "come to Jesus" moment, no dramatic conversion. My desire to be a Christian came in the day-to-day witness of those who were a part of the ministry teams that helped raise me. I am so grateful for the investment they made in my life many years ago.

After two years as a school music teacher, my life changed when God called me to ministry the first time. Those who had walked with me through my childhood faith journey brought me to a place where I was ready to hear God's call to ministry. I entered the Southern Baptist Theological Seminary to study church music with the clear thought that I would become a minister of music. Why a minister of music? Because my own minister of music had mentored me and guided me during my formative years. It was because of him that I was able to understand God's first call on my life.

For the past 40 years, however, I have lived a much different ministry life than I had planned for myself in those early days. Ministry has taken curves and detours that I could have never foreseen at the beginning. During the time I was a seminary student, I met my future husband. When we made the decision to get married, I shared with him my desire to serve in ministry with him—not separately from him. This promise was a call just as strong as my personal call to ministry. To raise our children together in the same church was also important to me.

I must say that this decision to serve with, instead of separately from, my husband has at times created some very difficult circumstances. My ministry life has been lived during the time of changing roles for women. I have found that in most of the churches we have served, I was the first "preacher's wife" who didn't do things in the traditional way. I wanted to be a minister, but I was the "preacher's wife." There were so many questions. How do you balance the two roles? Can a church have both a husband and wife on the same staff?

In today's world, shared ministry is more common, but it was not the case as we began our ministry lives in the 1980s. In our years of marriage we have served six different churches. Each time we moved to a new church, a new place of service, I would wait to discover which ministry area God might be calling me to. By waiting and listening for God, I found that my ministry was different in every church. To be honest, at the time that was very hard for me. But, through it all, God has always been by my side. Looking back, God's hand has been evident in every decision and every place of service. It has meant that I have had the chance to be a minister in almost all church ministry areas—children, youth, senior adults, and music. Each opportunity has provided a way to know the church intimately and to become comfortable ministering in each specialized area. I have learned that I need to trust God instead of myself. For 30 years I lived as an example of the continuous call of God to ministry.

And then, God surprised me. In February 2007 I was co-leading a women's retreat. In a time of personal prayer, I had my own Damascus Road experience. I found myself, on a cold and gray February day, sitting on the porch of a cabin in an Alabama state park. At this time in my life I felt as if I was wandering in a ministry desert with no sure destination. I was serving God, but something seemed not quite right in my ministry. As I was praying, I felt God speaking to me, giving me a new and different call—a call to pastoral ministry. I did not hear an audible voice, but I heard God's voice. It was as clear and sure as if I had actually heard God speaking.

Never in all my years of ministry had I ever considered being a pastor. But the call was too clear and too specific to ignore. I was shaken to my core. Later that afternoon I returned home and immediately shared this call with my husband. How did he respond? With the words, "Well, go do it!" He never wavered, never questioned if I had lost my mind, never asked how my call would affect his call and his ministry. In 2008 I entered seminary a second time at McAfee School of Theology, preparing to follow God's new call on my life. I had more questions than answers, but I only knew to trust that God had the answers waiting, if I would only follow this fresh call.

For three years I enveloped myself in a new seminary experience. I was surrounded by bright young adults who wrapped their arms around me and were the face of Jesus to me. They encouraged and supported my new call. And then I graduated, ready to follow this call into new ministry possibilities as a pastor. But it didn't happen. The next three years I searched diligently, but, over and over again, I was turned down, or not even heard. To be honest, the situation made me question my call. Had I really heard God that morning in February?

Then, out of the blue, I received a phone call from a friend whom I hadn't spoken to in at least 25 years. Would I consider interviewing for a position as an interim pastor? Over the next week, God was clearly in the middle of an opportunity that I would have never thought about, in a denomination I had never heard of.

Now, I have been a pastor in that denomination for about five years. As I look back over my life, I can see that God has been preparing me every step of the way.

Through my initial call that came out of a lifetime of Christian mentors who believed in me, to my second "Damascus Road" call, to my call to wait, and finally to my call as a pastor in a wonderful church, I have been blessed to see and experience a myriad of different ways that God can call each one of us. My prayer is that I will continue listening, maybe even for something new. Who knows?

I have always known that God is a God of surprises. Never has that been more evident than it is in my life today as I reflect on my call. My own story of God's calling is one that is ever changing, ever growing, ever surprising, and a perfect example of two different callings, separated by 33 years.

After serving in various ministry roles for more than 30 years and on church staffs in North and South Carolina, Tennessee, and Kentucky, Jane Hull followed a new call from God into the pastorate. She currently serves as the pastor of Union Christian Church (Disciples of Christ) in Watkinsville, Ga., where she lives with her husband, David.

The Story of My Call

William Hull

The sacred story we tell includes not only what Christ did for his earliest disciples but also what he continues to do for us today. Therefore, I want to tell you my story because it discloses some of the ways in which I have experienced the reality of Christ. Though mine is no Damascus Road drama such as Paul's, its very ordinariness may carry the suggestion that your story is worth telling as well.

When Paul started to tell his story, he went back to before he was born (Gal. 1:15), and so must I. My parents came from the red clay of central Alabama where their parents eked out a meager existence in the cruel aftermath of the Civil War. As a child, I frequently visited the "home place," my grandparents' little farm a few miles down a nameless road from a post office crossroads in Coosa County called Titus, Alabama. There was no central heating for warmth, only a fireplace in each bedroom and a wood stove in the kitchen; no plumbing for baths, only a washbasin filled by buckets of water brought from a nearby spring; no electricity for light, only kerosene lamps that cast eerie shadows in the twilight.

In that Spartan setting where life was lived close to its elemental forces, religion was serious business. Brother Hughes came over from Clanton every fourth Sunday to preach in the one-room Providence Baptist Church. The men sat on one side, where coffee cans were judiciously placed to receive well-aimed streams of "chawin' tobacco" juice; and the women sat on the other side, covered from head to toe in dresses made from flour sacks with only a cardboard fan furnished by the friendly funeral director to combat the stifling summer heat.

Shortly after World War I, my parents transplanted this rural heritage of unwavering faith to the young city of Birmingham. No sooner was I born than the Great Depression that dominated the 1930s devastated my father's real estate business, requiring our family to flee for shelter to a chicken farm run by a bachelor friend who offered us a roof over our heads in exchange for my mother's cooking and housekeeping.

Despite these deprivations, there was never any question that we would be in church every time the doors opened. My earliest memory of worship at the Hunter Street Baptist Church is that of lying with my head in my mother's lap and my feet in the lap of the lady next to her, while both of them fanned to keep me from becoming restless.

When I was nine years old, we moved and began to attend the Central Park Baptist Church in Birmingham. The pastor's wife was our Sunday School departmental superintendent who, in response to many a childish prank, never failed to let me know that she was praying for my urgently needed salvation! During my tenth or eleventh year, the annual revival meeting began to claim some of my schoolmates. I remember sitting one afternoon on the back steps of our home, resting from play with a little girl from across the street. Without a trace of self-consciousness, she described how she had recently "gone forward" to profess her faith, then asked with disarming candor, "When are you going to join the church?" I quickly mumbled something about attending to that matter shortly, then changed the subject so that she could not tell just how wildly my heart was beating. It had taken only her simple question to let me know beyond any shadow of doubt that I had been claimed, that it was only a matter of time before I would seek the waters of baptism as she had done.

The decision was made, as I remember, on a Tuesday or Wednesday evening of the next year's revival series. Like so many, I cannot now recollect who was preaching or anything about the sermon. But I do know that it was my own decision, freely made, with a remarkable awareness of its ultimacy granted my tender years. Looking back, more than a half-century later, I would have to say that, even though the commitment was entirely uncoerced, it was shaped to a large extent by a faith that had first dwelt in my parents and grandparents (2 Tim. 1:5)

Shortly after becoming a Christian I entered adolescence, that awkward transitional stage when one tries to put away childish things in order to become an adult (1 Cor. 13:11). My churchgoing habits were too deeply entrenched to be dislodged, even by the ceaseless experimentation of this impulsive period in life. But I did shift from the front pews to the back, and began to sit by girls instead of boys, to whom I passed cute little notes written on the back of offering envelopes during the pastor's sermons. After Sunday School, before the worship service began, some of my peers would slip down to the corner drugstore, but I found this furtive escape entirely too daring to risk the displeasure of my parents, even though they never tried to keep me on a tight leash.

As I reflect back on those early teen years, it at first seems strange that I made so little of my newly found Christian commitment. Even though I had been thoroughly saturated in the environment of faith for a dozen years, the climactic exhilaration of baptism seemed to lead nowhere. The next half-dozen years I merely marked time, responding to what was provided and expected. Oh, I made the required meetings, glanced at the Sunday School quarterly, and put a little money in my offering envelope, but, in truth, I was letting the church carry me while I merely capitulated, half-willingly and half-reluctantly, to its routines. To be honest, I was getting, not giving; I was holding on, not helping out; most importantly, the great gift of new life in Christ was lying dormant rather than developing into maturity.

I have often wondered about this pause in my spiritual pilgrimage. Someone has said that grace grows best in winter. If so, this parenthesis in my pilgrimage was a time for the seed to grow secretly, waiting for the warmth of springtime to burst into bud and then into bloom.

Once I had shifted from a holding pattern to a growing pattern, I became actively involved in the ministries of the church. One childhood elective had been serious training in music, first the violin and then choral groups, hence it was easy to turn these talents toward leading "singspiration" or directing the BSU choir. With broadening experience came a clear assessment of my gifts. Even though I had been doing well in pre-med and was virtually assured of a slot in medical school, it would not be true to say that this vocational option was fulfilling my highest dreams. In October 1949, when a junior in college, I attended the statewide Baptist Student Union convention at Shocco Springs—half-impulsively I must confess—primarily in hopes of seeing some of my "old flames" from high school days now studying on other campuses. But what I really saw during that weekend were college youth like myself giving their lives to Christian service in ways that I had never dared consider. By the time of the final service on Sunday morning, my decision was made to enter a church-related vocation, a commitment that had been growing within me even while I was refusing to recognize it.

Entering the ministry was for me a leap in the dark. No one in my family had been a preacher. I had not talked with anyone about this possibility, nor did I have any idea what it would entail in terms of training or skills. When I wrote my parents of the decision, it took them completely by surprise. And yet it was the most certain thing I have ever done, a resolve from which I have never wavered. If my conversion was by God's grace mediated through family, my vocation calling was by that same grace given, as Paul put it, apart from conferring with flesh and blood (Gal. 1:15-16). When I was a child, God worked through the earthly continuities with which I was familiar, but, when I became a man, he must have felt that I was ready for a crisis that would turn my life in an entirely new direction determined by his initiative.

Once the call was heard, I responded much like Abraham who "went out, not knowing where he was to go" (Heb. 11:8 RSV). Immediately I changed schools and majors, from pre-med at the University of Alabama to religion at Howard College (now Samford University). At Samford I was initiated into the larger Baptist fraternity and, even more important, found my future wife, who was studying for a church-related vocation in religious education. I also served my first student pastorate, a country church near Wetumpka, Ala., where patient folk loved me dearly despite my amateurish efforts that bordered on ministerial malpractice.

Upon graduating, I was off to Southern Seminary in Louisville, Ky., to complete my theological training at both the professional and graduate levels. During those years I served two more student pastorates, was married, and both of our children were born. Seminary opened to me a vast world of theological thought that has been endlessly fascinating ever since, particularly in my chosen specialty of New Testament interpretation that I stayed to teach at Southern for 20 years. I was also provided opportunities for administrative leadership at every level from departmental chairman to chief academic officer as provost.

During those decades of service in our denomination's oldest seminary, I was constantly speaking in a wide variety of Baptist churches and denominational conferences, which led to the frequent question of whether my first preference was preaching, teaching, or administration. The truth is that I have always found great fulfillment in all three avenues of service. My vocation has made me an incurable workaholic, not because extra effort would lead to additional prominence or financial reward, but because every facet of the ministry is so fulfilling! If I were independently wealthy, I would gladly pay someone to let me do exactly what I have done during all my adult life.

The consuming love for every aspect of ministry was doubtless a factor prompting me to consider the possibility of a call to the First Baptist Church in Shreveport, La., for the pastoral role is the most comprehensive position in the Christian ministry. There I found endless opportunities to preach and teach and administer, as well as to work with many individuals, families, and civic groups. Over the period of a dozen years (1975–1987) I formed the most intimate relationships imaginable with those who turned to me to help them find the deepest meaning of the great ventures of life: birth, marriage, family, divorce, work, disease, death. My congregation was filled with influential members, and, through them, I was privileged to become significantly involved in the life of the city and its surrounding region.

Then why did I consider returning to my hometown of Birmingham and to my alma mater of Samford University after an absence of 36 years? Partly because of the compelling vision of its energetic new president. Partly because the university stood poised on the threshold of a new level of usefulness in its long and colorful history. Partly because work as provost would permit me to gather up all my efforts as theologian, seminarian, and pastor and seek to integrate them in the cause of Christian higher education. In a phrase, I returned to help build a community in which faith and learning enrich each other. In the face of skepticism in the academy and anti-intellectualism in the church, I wanted to demonstrate afresh that, at their best, education is good for religion, and religion is good for education.

My chosen path has not been easy. I have experienced a full measure of setbacks and defeats. But even in failure, I know that I am slowly but surely being saved: from depending upon my own strength to depending upon God's strength, from self-centered isolation to community-centered fellowship, from conformity to the world to conformity to Christ. Such is my story: of a grace that was already waiting as soon as I was ready to receive it, of a growth that shattered my inertia and lethargy of spirit and set me on a pilgrimage toward maturity, of a gratitude that I can spend my days helping you to live out a story worth telling to others!

William Hull (1930–2013) served as a professor and administrator at Southern Seminary; senior pastor of First Baptist Church of Shreveport, La.; provost at Samford University; and theologian in residence at Mountain Brook Baptist Church in Birmingham, Ala. This call story is an excerpt of a biographical sermon included in Dr. Hull's book, Harbingers of Hope.

The Location of God's Call

Charles Foster Johnson

When I was born, my father's family had been Methodist for several generations already. So, I grew up in a fairly typical Methodist church of the Deep South, liturgical and formal in style and order. I remember serving as an acolyte in the Gadsden Street United Methodist Church in Pensacola, Fla., as a little boy, leading the processional of minister and choir into the sanctuary for Sabbath worship, feeling spiffy in my starched white robe. I learned early on that church was important and that it held a place of importance even for the littlest and the least in the community.

At 15, my mother's family heritage, marked by a more rawboned rural religious sensibility, won out. We joined the Baptist church, and my father and I were baptized together. The wonderful First Baptist Church of Pensacola was huge and energetic, not the sedate environment of my Methodist upbringing. Folks moved and laughed and sang their hearts out in worship. The stillness and quietness of my Methodist upbringing, important values of devotion to be sure, were missing among these Baptist folks. The pastor, Jim Pleitz, presided over the entire community with humor and dynamism. People actually pronounced out loud their blessing and affirmation of God's goodness with hearty exclamations of "Amen!" The blessing of it all was rich and deep for me. I became involved in the church's many projects of love and outreach in the community. It was impressed upon my adolescent mind the fundamental importance of service to our fellow human beings, as Christ so frequently taught. The point didn't escape me: faith is something one *does*.

This Baptist understanding of mission was underscored even more forcefully in my experience at Mississippi College. I became involved in student ministries that were ordered around two things: Scripture study and acts of service. The one could not be successfully done without the other. They were inextricably linked. Both required the fellowship, partnership, and prayers of other Christians. I hardly knew the concept of discipleship at the time, but someone gave me a powerful book with the term in the title, by an author whose name I could not pronounce. Dietrich Bonhoeffer's *The Cost of Discipleship* rocked my world.

One day well into the second semester of my sophomore year, Mississippi College's Baptist Student Union director Bradley Pope called me into his office to inform me about a summer mission opportunity in Washington D.C., a faith and politics internship sponsored by Riverside Baptist and St. Dominic's Catholic churches, two congregations just several blocks from the mall southwest of the Capitol. It was the location in our nation's capital that got my attention more than the mission itself. I was a political science major, preparing to practice law. What better place for an aspiring attorney, about to immerse himself in the preparatory subjects of his major field of study, than the seat of the law itself? So, I accepted the internship.

My daily responsibility revolved around two major spheres of activity: government and ministry. In the morning I visited government officials in various positions of the three branches. In the afternoon I conducted a day camp for poor children in the nearby housing projects. The juxtaposition of these two divergent spheres of human activity, literally bumping up against each other geographically, was a point of deep spiritual reflection for me at a very formative stage of my adult development.

The year was 1977. President Jimmy Carter occupied the White House and brought his southern-ness to town with him. Washington was still a manageably small city at that time. It seems impossible today for a couple of neighborhood churches to have such personal connection with so many powerful people of government, but Riverside and St. Dominic's knew many folks of prominent positions in the executive, legislative, and judicial branches. The church leaders arranged visits for me with these individuals: Senate and congressional leaders, Cabinet secretaries, agency heads, White House and Supreme Court staffers. My mornings were scheduled daily with these conversations around the role and function of government, the political issues of the day, the nature of democratic institutions, and the meaning of America. It was enthralling for a young collegian.

The afternoon experience with the children of the low-income housing projects was a light year away, though only separated by several blocks from the addresses of Washington power. In the late 1960s and early 1970s, urban renewal in our large cities saw the construction of blocks upon blocks of high-rise apartment complexes for poor people, their tenement housing having been purchased by the federal government from rent barons and demolished. These monolithic and numbingly de-personalized structures were designed to relieve the poor of their inadequate housing and substandard living conditions. They did not. What resulted instead was a colossal failure in social experimentation. The poor became warehoused in multi-story high-rises that triggered a proliferation of additional pathologies: drug trafficking, prostitution, gang activity, etc. Most of these housing units were occupied by single-parent families, almost always a young mother. Almost all of these folks were unemployed—subsistence living.

My ministry consisted of conducting meaningful and enriching summer programs for the children of these housing projects. We arranged games, crafts, swimming in the public pool, and field trips to the local museums and libraries, while the neighborhood churches provided a daily meal and religious education. During the evenings Riverside's Pastor Bob Troutman and St. Dominic's Father Bill Newman would engage me in theological, economic, and political reflection about the day's events; the conversations in the morning with the nation's power brokers; and the interactions in the afternoon with our nation's poorest children. For 10 weeks in that summer of 1977, these two groups of people engaged my thoughts and perspectives.

Finishing the internship in August, I returned home and prepared to enter my junior year of pre-law studies. But it wasn't the captains of government that commanded my attention.

It was those kids. God had staked a claim on me through those inner-city ghetto children. It wasn't the buttoned-down and crisp-suited leaders on Capitol Hill that captured my faith imagination that summer, but the snotty-nosed, foul-mouthed kids in the projects. My calling didn't come from the alabaster edifices, but from the dingy and crumbling apartment complexes in their shadows.

On the Sunday before my return to Mississippi College for the fall semester, I responded to the invitation from Pastor Pleitz at the conclusion of the evening worship service, and "surrendered to full-time Christian service," as the language of the day described that profound vocational decision. It was a moment of abundant blessing and affirmation. I stood next to my pastor as he presented me to the congregation, his arm draped in endorsement around my shoulders. In the colorful phrase of a Baptist preacher, he said, "Beloved, I feel the gates of hell shake tonight because of this young man's decision." A gracious hyperbole, but I didn't feel anything that dramatic. It seemed natural and effortless, like coming to the supper table when my mama called out the back door for me as a boy. But I know now that my pastor was right: hell cowers at a life claimed by the call of God.

That fall at Mississippi College I entered youth ministry—a typical first-stage expression of an incipient call—first with the Northminster Baptist Church of Jackson, Miss., under the pastoral leadership of the venerable John Claypool and later with the First Baptist Church of Pontotoc, Miss., under Gordon Sansing. Both of these superb pastors gently nurtured my instincts for ministry in formative ways. Both of these churches sealed my call with their congregational affirmation, Northminister through licensing and Pontotoc through ordination.

After college I entered Southern Baptist Theological Seminary in Louisville, Ky., and soon thereafter assumed my first pastorate with the West Point Baptist Church of Matanzas, Ky. From there I served the First Baptist Church of Albany, Ky. These two rural churches honed my skills for ministry in the first decade of my call. In 1989 I was called to the Second Baptist Church of Lubbock, Texas, a progressive, university town faith community that determined the missional and theological direction of my ministry. In 2001 I became the senior pastor of the huge Trinity Baptist Church of San Antonio, a ministry that challenged my administrative capacities and deepened my understanding of what Martin Luther King Jr. called the "beloved community."

The next several years constituted a period of transition, taking me to several wonderful short-term charges: two years of teaching preaching at McAfee School of Theology of Mercer University in Atlanta, followed by three interim pastorates: Immanuel Baptist Church of Nashville, Broadway Baptist Church of Fort Worth, and First Baptist Church of Brownwood, Texas. In 2010 I began Bread Fellowship of Fort Worth where I serve today. In 2013 I founded Pastors for Texas Children, a social justice ministry mobilizing the faith community for public education support and advocacy. This organization now has offshoots in Oklahoma, Kentucky, Tennessee, and Mississippi, and will soon launch in a number of other southern and midwestern states.

I'm now in the 42nd year of my call. It has beckoned me to a wonderful ministry with great people who, along with my dear wife Jana, have been Christ incarnate for me. I've recognized its accent and tenor and tone each time it spoke on the journey, just as recognizable and familiar as when it announced itself so compellingly long ago.

I think of that announcement often, and wonder if I've made good on the claim it registered so deeply on me that summer through those children. I think of them, their innocent capacity to love not yet impaired by a cruel world, their little hands running endlessly through my straight hair that so fascinated them. I find myself still seduced at times by the alabaster power brokers always only a few short steps away, still charmed by their flirtations, especially now that my call takes me to their corridors to advocate for the children who languish nearby in their shadow. Those 1977 children are middle-aged now, and if statistics tell us anything, are poor themselves, imprisoned, diseased, and devoid of the justice God promises for every human. Many are dead. Did they ever know how special and significant they were? Did it ever occur to them that they transformed a life? Did they ever realize they were the voice of God?

Bonhoeffer chillingly wrote, "When Christ calls a man, He bids him come and die"—another pastoral hyperbole. But his slam-bang whack up side our head is correct. The calling of Christ is to end the life we thought we wanted for ourselves and to begin the life that God envisions for us. What we think is in store for us is nothing more than fiddling with our nets, but he walks by and tells us to drop them and to walk with him, because he has something much better for us. Even though it's crazy, we say yes to that call. We recognize the voice, and we follow it because it's so sure and steady and full of love that we cannot help it. We answer it. And that makes all the difference.

Charles Foster Johnson is pastor of Bread Fellowship in Fort Worth, Texas, and founder and executive director of Pastors for Texas Children.

The Journey from New York to Florida

Joseph V. LaGuardia

"You don't want to get married?" This was the question my aunt asked me when I announced to the family that I was going to be a minister. My family—Italian, all of us—assumed that ministry meant priesthood, and priesthood meant celibacy. Never mind God, the pope, and the one, holy Catholic Church—the priesthood was a threat to the family line. As an only son, I was to carry on my father's namesake. The only other time I saw a face as frightened as my aunt's was when I told my mother that my wife and I were not having more children. Apparently, God created men in my family to serve only one purpose.

My aunt's assumptions about my life are not as odd as one might assume. In fact, when I tell people I am a pastor, some call me "Father" or "Padre." A few have called me "Rabbi." Still others have asked if my wife wears a hijab. Several people from India asked what part of India I come from. I am a religious and ethnic enigma.

Barbara Brown Taylor once wrote that the call to serve God is a call to become fully human. That said, I am an Italian from New York, and I am an ordained Southern Baptist minister. It does not seem right, but that's what it means to be fully human to me. How did I get from there to here?

I was born to a blue-collar family in Staten Island, New York, when the island was facing a Protestant revival. Several church start-ups in the late 1960s capitalized on the waning influence of the Catholic Church among Italians and persuaded people to go Protestant. This was a time of economic hardship, and solace was hard to come by. One of those church-starts was Gateway Cathedral founded by the Reverend Dr. Daniel Mercaldo. He encouraged people to have a personal relationship with Jesus. He inspired people to read the Bible on their own. He delivered an empowering message for Staten Islanders.

My parents visited Gateway and, by my first birthday, Dr. Mercaldo baptized them by immersion. It was 1979, only a few months after I had been baptized as an infant in the Catholic Church. My mother did that to make sure I was not going to hell, in case I failed to reach the age of accountability and be baptized by Dr. Mercaldo too. When people ask me if I grew up Catholic, I tell them I did, at least for the first year of my life.

My parents explained to the rest of our family the difference between Catholics and Protestants. They explained why they did not attend Mass or have their children take First

Communion. They engaged in culture wars and promoted the Christian Coalition, of which Gateway Cathedral was a part. Why my aunt did not understand ministry by the time I announced my intention to become a pastor is beyond me; my father advocated for his brand of Christianity for nearly three decades. He had encouraged her to have a personal relationship with Jesus, to ignore the priest, and to read the Bible for herself. This experiential, "Bible-believing" faith best explains how I got from there to here. I took this notion of personal relationship and Bible reading seriously in my childhood, and my love of the Christian faith grounded me.

There was one Christmas—I must have been about 5 years of age—when I came home from church with a clear conviction that believers were to read and obey the Bible. I noticed that my older sister, a voracious reader, did not read her Bible. I snuck into her room, got her Bible, and wrapped it in wrapping paper. I put a tag on it that said, "To Gina, love Jesus," and stuck it under the tree. When she opened it Christmas day, she said, "It's just my Bible," and I responded, "I wrapped it for you because you never read it." Even then, I knew God's Word was a gift.

We moved to Florida a few years later, and my parents had a bit of a church crisis. They tried to find a church that matched the charisma and hospitality of Gateway. They sought out all manner of worship services, but nothing seemed to fit. They agreed to attend church with my uncle at the First Baptist Church of Perrine. This was my first introduction to Baptist life. It was a rather large congregation. My father and sister helped in the audio-visual ministry, running television cameras every Sunday. My Sunday School class and youth group were full, though impersonal and overwhelming. I did not talk much when I attended, and most Sundays I slept on the pew, my head in my mother's lap, during the sermon.

It was in one of those youth group gatherings, however, that I heard the gospel as if for the first time. The youth pastor explained it well: how we all fall short of God's glory and we need to repent and ask Jesus into our hearts. The leaders gave us tracts, and after reading mine every night I attended the youth group meeting the following Wednesday and went forward to accept Jesus as my Savior. It was mystifying because, on the one hand, I thought I would feel euphoria for "accepting Jesus," but, on the other hand, I believed that I had a personal relationship with Jesus all along. For some reason, the call felt much more complicated than the tract described, and much more endearing than a simple five-minute prayer and response at youth group. It was all very confusing.

Describing the mysteries of childhood, in her book *An American Childhood*, Annie Dillard wrote, "Children. . . wake up and find themselves here, discover themselves to have been here along. They wake like sleepwalkers, in full stride; they wake like people brought back from cardiac arrest or from drowning" (p. 11). This is how I came to know Christ, not with one decision, but over time. Christ was familiar, personal; but, when I walked the aisle in youth group, it was as if I was waking up to what I had known for a long time.

Awakening, according to Dillard, happens in bits and pieces, slipping back and forth between infancy and adolescence; yet, children never really become free from who they are in the moment. The youth pastor told us we were free in Jesus, but I always felt too stuck in my own fragile skin to know whether it was true. I became a bona fide Christian, but I was still Italian, northern, dark-skinned, and different. I still fell asleep during the sermons, and I relished the days when my parents chose not to attend church because First Baptist was not Gateway, thus affording me time to watch Sunday morning cartoons. I slid back and forth.

Eventually, I grew up. I settled on the idea that my decision was not a one-time occurrence, but the result of a daily commitment to something beyond myself, even when I only had myself to live with. I later learned that the great Reformer Martin Luther experienced a similar wrestling match with his own sense of sin and awkward relationship to Christ. According to history, Luther experienced liberation and sparked the Reformation only when he broke away from the church of his youth.

In high school I told my parents I needed a new church. I started attending a charismatic Presbyterian church that prioritized discipleship and ministry, and within a month I was hooked. I attended retreats, found ways to help my youth pastor, and tried my hand at teaching Bible study to middle school students. I darkened the doors of that church most days, and I wanted to learn as much as possible. I read the Bible and my relationship to Christ became participatory. I decided to attend a Baptist college and major in ministry. I knew that was to be my career—as Martin Luther once said, "I can do no other."

In my third year of college I visited my New Testament professor and asked him how I might know whether God was calling me to be a minister or if this was all a big joke. He cited Frederick Buechner and said that my calling is where my deepest passion meets the world's greatest needs. It was not just a career, but a giving of one life to serve the lives of others. "Can you do that, LaGuardia?" he asked.

I said that I was able and willing, but I still attended the Presbyterian Church. And, although the church served as the incubator for my faith and provided the sacred space for my wife and me to wed, it was not the denomination to which I committed. After graduation it was time to move on once again, to grow up rather than slip back into adolescence. I enrolled in a Baptist seminary in Atlanta, got a position at a small Baptist church, and served as a chaplain at a Baptist retirement high-rise in Decatur, Ga. I finally felt at home in my own skin, though it was difficult for others to accept me as one of their own—after all, I still had a northern accent and an arsenal of Italian colloquialisms. God called me to ministry—in that I was confident—but it seemed nothing short of what Lillian Daniel and Martin Copenhaver call an "odd and wondrous calling."

A good pastor shepherds her flock from the inside out, but when your last name is hard to pronounce—like mine surely is—it is difficult for people to get past the outside and go deeply in. It is hard enough for pastors to make friends, and if you live in the South but are not southern born and bred, it is even more challenging. In those rare moments when I feel displaced—as Harlem poet James Weldon Johnson describes it, "A motherless child, a long way from home"—I return to my roots: This is not about religion, but a personal relationship to

Christ. It is about Holy Scripture, to which I am inevitably drawn time and again. I may have left the theology of Gateway behind, but evangelicalism still informs the very heart of who I am.

My dream had always been to preach in a large-steeple church. In 2016 my dream came true when I answered the call to become the pastor of First Baptist Church in Vero Beach, Fla. Unlike Atlanta, Vero Beach is a community that is as odd as I. Although there are many natives, much of the population is made up of retirees from the North. I can preach southern, but when I crack a New York colloquial, at least half of my congregation understands it. I can dig deep into God's Word as any compliant Southern Baptist ought to do, but I can also speak of labor unions and urban politics with people who wrestle with such "Yankee concerns." I can order shrimp and grits and sacrifice the quality of neither ingredient. I visit with folks who remember listening to New York Mayor Fiorello LaGuardia read the funny pages to children over the radio. And, at the end of the day, when I return to my family and we sit around playing Monopoly, I tell my children that they too can have a personal relationship with Jesus, read the Bible for themselves, and hear Christ's whisper if they are awakened enough to their surroundings. It is not the typical picture of a Southern Baptist preacher, but it is fully human.

Joseph V. LaGuardia is the pastor of First Baptist Church of Vero Beach, Fla. He and his family enjoy the beach, reading, and playing board games. The author of several books, his work has also appeared on BaptistSpirituality.com and EthicsDaily.com and in The Rockdale Citizen *and* USA Today.

Your Servant Is Listening

Ron Lyles

We make provision for it with words such as, "I am not available to take your call right now," or, "I'm sorry that I missed your call. Your call is very important to me. Please leave your name and number." We detest missing a telephone call. That is the reason why we are reluctant to turn our phones off when sitting in worship, in a memorial service, or in an airplane seat. God's call to Christian service is one call that must not be missed.

My parents married soon after my dad returned from serving in the United States Navy during World War II. Dad was a high school history teacher in Decatur, Texas, when I joined the family as their second son. (A native Texan, I have lived in Texas my entire life, so every place mentioned in this article is in Texas.)

Both of my parents grew up in families that lived out their faith in Jesus both at home and through involvement in church. As a result, the family that they began and shaped was a family of faith, fully involved in the life of a church family wherever we lived. The first church nursery bed in which I was placed was in the First Baptist Church of Decatur.

Several years later, Dad was teaching in Snyder in West Texas when the First Baptist Church there held a revival. The evangelist proclaimer for the week was a professor from Wayland Baptist College in Plainview. I was four years old at the time. Since both my brother and I had the chicken pox that week, Mom and Dad attended the revival on alternate nights. By the closing service on Sunday morning, all four of us were able to be present. At the conclusion of that service my father went forward and declared that he believed God was calling him into the Christian ministry. The declaration of that call and resultant career move changed everything.

From that time, I became the son of a seminary student and, ultimately, a Baptist pastor. While Dad was still attending Southwestern Baptist Theological Seminary in Fort Worth, he accepted a call to become the part-time pastor of Antioch Baptist Church near Leonard in northeast Texas.

For the summer revival of 1956, the pews were moved outside and we worshiped "under the stars." God spoke to me during one of the services, and I responded publicly during the invitation. Dad assisted me in the decision to invite Jesus to be the Lord of my life. Making that initial decision to follow Jesus so early in my life was only possible through the cooperative effort of my parents and the churches they attended. Both taught me that God loved me.

Dad finished his seminary studies and became the pastor of Temple Baptist Church in Tyler. In the summer of 1962 my Royal Ambassadors group from that church participated in RA Camp at the Pineywoods Baptist Encampment between Groveton and Corrigan. On the last night of the camp, after a "foreign missionary" had shared a message, God spoke to me again.

I was standing next to my best friend and baseball teammate, Bill Durham. Billy was the shortstop for the best double-play combination in the Tyler Little League (I was the second baseman for it). I turned to my friend and declared that we should go forward and make a decision. He replied, "No one should go down there unless he feels like he is supposed to." That was how I felt, and I did go down there.

That night I declared to a camp counselor that I believed God was calling me into Christian service to become a pastor. When I returned home, I met with my dad/pastor in his office. His counsel to me was that if you think you can be happy doing anything else in life, then do it. He did not want me to pursue this ministry direction if my motivation was to make Mom and him happy. He sometimes described pastors he knew as "Daddy called and Momma sent," rather than being called by God. I assured Dad that I made my own decision, as certain as a 12-year-old boy can be, in response to a call from God.

With his encouragement, I shared my decision with the church family at Temple Baptist Church. They promised to pray for me and support me in that important life decision.

Dad and I continued our conversation over the next several months about what that "call to ministry" meant. He then surprised me by suggesting that he wanted to help me prepare and deliver a sermon to the Temple Baptist congregation. He allowed me to select the text, and then he helped me tremendously in the preparation of my first sermon.

I selected 1 Samuel 3:1-21, the story about Samuel and Eli, to be the biblical text. I determined to use that story because I felt somewhat of a connection to Samuel. Both of us experienced a call from God as a young boy. (With that one feature in common, the comparison ends of course.)

On Sunday evening, January 27, 1963, I used that text as the basis of a message titled, "The Man God Uses." I was 12 years old, and the sermon was 12 minutes long. The congregation was very gracious and affirming, especially grateful for its brevity. I still have my handwritten notes of the outline of the sermon, scribbled on a piece of my dad's church stationery.

I have always been grateful for my father's wise counsel and guidance when I initially shared with him my sense of being called by God to serve in ministry. I have had very few times of professional disappointments that were strong enough to cause me to question whether I was really doing what God wanted me to do. During those few times, however, it was the certainty of the memory that God had indeed spoken to me and called me to Christian ministry that provided me the confidence to continue faithfully in my ministry journey.

Consistently, church congregations have been a vital part of my living out God's call upon my life. During my high school years, I had the privilege of preaching on "Youth Sundays" when they were scheduled at my own church and other congregations. In the providence of

God, in 1966, Dad was called to be the pastor of First Baptist Church in Decatur, my first "home church nursery."

The Decatur church licensed me to gospel ministry in May of 1968, two weeks before I graduated from high school. My dad/pastor placed the presentation Bible in my hand. When my wife and I attended the 50th reunion gathering of my graduating class in April of 2018, I had the privilege of preaching at the same church, 50 years after it affirmed me for ministry. What a special joy.

During my first three years at Dallas Baptist University I had the privilege of preaching almost every Sunday in a supply role at small, rural churches while the pastor was away. I was finishing my junior year in college when, in May 1971, Dad asked me to preach at one of the small churches in the Red River Baptist Association where he was then serving as the director of missions. The church was inbetween pastors.

One month after I preached at Brookston Baptist Church, the congregation invited me to become their pastor. I accepted their invitation and was ordained to gospel ministry by that fellowship. From that time, I have had the privilege of serving four churches as pastor, the last 37 years as senior pastor of South Main Baptist Church in Pasadena, Texas. Each of these congregations has been gracious in allowing me to live out my call by God using God's gifted-ness to resource that call.

In each of the congregations where I have served, I have always communicated to our adults, students, and preteens the need to be sensitive to the call of God to salvation and sensi-tive to the call of God to Christian ministry and service. At South Main we have sought to foster a healthy church context and culture in which persons respond to and are nurtured in that call.

Several years ago I determined to have a service in which we celebrated that context and culture. We called it a "Celebration of Ministry" Sunday. We sent letters to more than 60 persons/couples who had grown up in our church. These were men and women who were serving in ministry (or the spouse of one who served). They included pastors, missionaries, college and seminary professors, music ministers, education ministers, student ministers, and children's ministers. It was a great day. One of my sons was among the group with whom we celebrated their role in ministry.

The reason I love the Bible story that served as the text for my first sermon is that it contains all of the necessary components to the process in which God calls persons to serve others in Christian ministry. Of course, no one can be called by God without the presence of God—the one who takes the initiative and extends the invitation to listen. I believe it was God who called me to proclaim the good news of Jesus.

In addition to God who calls, we have someone who is willing to listen to God and receive an assignment: the boy named Samuel. Samuel was privileged to have parents (Hannah and Elkhanah) who placed their son at the sanctuary at Shiloh. God called Samuel within the context of community—the community of biological family and the community of the people called Israel. I am grateful that God extended the call to me within the context of two communities: my parents who were committed Jesus followers and churches that taught me, nurtured me, and allowed me to live out my calling in pastoral ministry.

Finally, God used Eli the priest as a mentor to guide Samuel in the understanding of the fact that God was speaking to him. It was Eli who gave Samuel the instructions of how to respond to God and what to say. He advised Samuel to say, "Speak, LORD, for your servant is listening." I was blessed to have my dad as my Eli. He was the one who walked alongside me, guided and advised me, and helped me to understand the implications of God's call upon my life.

I have missed many telephone calls in my life, but I am grateful to the Lord Jesus that I did not miss the most important call in my life: God's call to Christian ministry. I do not believe that I could have been happy doing anything else except what I have been doing for more than 55 years, living out my call to Christian ministry.

A native Texan, Ron Lyles has been a pastor for almost 50 years. For 37 years he has served as the senior pastor of South Main Baptist Church in Pasadena, Texas, where he and his wife Brenda reared their four children.

"Emmanuel":
Someday He's Going to Preach

Emmanuel McCall

As early as age eight, I was aware of a "calling" to ministry. I was raised on a farm in Pennsylvania, and I can recall preaching to the chickens and pigs. I said nothing of this, and certainly not to my family.

By age 12, that inclination left me. I saw what the Valley Baptist Church had done to my adopted grandpa. He was the pastor. That church had an "annual call" meeting on the last Sunday of December. The pastor and his wife would be asked to leave the building, and the church would vote whether or not to invite him to continue. He was not invited back. As I observed, they treated him poorly. Maybe it was my affection for him, or maybe I just didn't understand some things the "old folk" were talking about. I just didn't like it.

I developed an interest in music. My Uncle Henry directed a jazz band. I went to one of the outdoor concerts in the park. Uncle Henry persuaded me to try the trombone. I did. I liked it. For the next four years that was my interest, but not my passion. Gnawing at my spirit was the call to ministry.

One evening I was husking corn in one of our fields after dark. (This was to prepare the corn for the winter crib long before modern farm equipment.) Oil lamps provided the light. That night I had a clear sense that ministry was to be my life calling. For me, the evening was euphoric.

I said nothing to my family but talked to our pastor Frank Waller. He greatly rejoiced for my calling, because he now had a "son" in whom he could vest himself. He had always wanted a son. He had five girls. He even gave the last two boy's names: "Frankie Elizabeth and Charles Sidney." (I don't think they ever forgave him for that.)

Pastor Waller thought that you "prepared by doing." Rather than letting me finish high school before beginning my preaching, he immediately set the time for my initial sermon: Nov. 5, 1950, 3:00 p.m. When I had finished my initial attempt at preaching, Rev. DeLane, my adopted grandfather, asked to speak.

When I was eight days old a ceremony was held in my parents' home, Rev. DeLane told the church. Following the Old Testament tradition of "blessing the baby," my parents gave our pastor the choice of naming me. He named me "Emmanuel Lemuel," and announced that someday I would preach. But the eight people in the room were sworn to secrecy; none were to tell me of the prediction. On the occasion of my first sermon, all eight of them were present. Rev. DeLane had them stand as he revealed the prophecy to the congregation. He saw my future. "Emmanuel," God with us; "Lemuel," the wisdom of Solomon.

Frank Waller gave me every opportunity for growth and development. I followed him on visits to the sick, to church meetings, to denominational and other public meetings. I preached often so that he could critique me. I helped with funerals and anything else he thought to be beneficial. He loved to fish. Often, our fishing trips became times of fatherly, pastoral advice.

When I finished high school Rev. Waller suggested that I go to the college and seminary he attended, Simmons University in Louisville, Ky. He did not know that in the years since he was last on campus, the school was foreclosed on. The only salvaged part was a theological institute that functioned to help those called to ministry but unable to attend an accredited institution.

When I arrived on campus, I was very disappointed. I called my pastor to give a status report. He advised me to stay with the school for one year. He wanted me to become familiar with Baptist doctrine as taught by the Simmons faculty. I did. It prepared me to attend the University of Louisville and later the Southern Baptist Theological Seminary.

This was the 1950s. Public schools were attempting "integration." The University of Louisville had just opened its doors. Even though "opened," some aspects were still "closed." The one salvific event at U. of L. was that the Baptist Student Union was "open." I and one other black student were sought and welcomed in.

My life at U. of L. was limited because I had to work in the afternoon and evenings to pay for school, as no scholarships were available. So, it was classes in the morning, one or two hours of fellowship at BSU, and then work. The brief time at BSU endeared me to young people who were ready to break the mold of segregation. They even defied the Long Run Baptist Association that sponsored the BSU when the association decided that non-whites could not attend. The students, along with the student director, Fred Witty, became my life on campus.

From 1954–1958, I was involved in all the BSU did across the state of Kentucky. I was the only black person in most instances. I was not trying to "crash" or "make a statement"—I just wanted to be involved. My white student friends encouraged me. Little did I know that God was using these experiences to prepare me for larger ministries.

At the same time that God was preparing me for God's future, God was also preparing the young lady I was dating to share in my future. Emma Marie was not on campus. She was one of the musicians at the church where I served as a student in ministry. She accompanied me to some of the events the BSU sponsored. In 1958 we married.

I began study at Southern Baptist Theological Seminary. My wife fit right in since we were the only blacks on campus. Both of us were becoming accustomed to life with Southern Baptists, both persons and the denomination.

When one answers the "call" to ministry, the "call" may include other "calls." I later found myself involved in a new direction of "call."

In January 1962 I was exiting the seminary library at the same time as Dr. John Claypool. We stopped to talk about the dreadful news of cities in crises over school integration. After lamenting the situation, John indicated that he had an idea. He invited me to go to the student lounge to discuss his idea. He felt that if we could ever get the black and white Baptists in Louisville talking to each other, we might avert the problems happening elsewhere.

For the next hour we discussed the "how to" of that task. John would find six white pastors, and I would find six black pastors. We would meet privately, trying to understand each other, our histories, our problems, our churches, our passions for justice, and our willingness to "move out" on God's mission. This we did. After four months we developed the Louisville Baptist Ministers Interracial Fellowship. Louisville was spared the turmoil of other cities. The group went on to become a model for interracial progress.

My sense of "call" had to make room for other ways God would use me. From 1968–1991, the focus of my ministry became identified with racial reconciliation through the Home Mission Board of the Southern Baptist Convention. Since then it has also included church starting, church development, 26 years of adjunct teaching at the Southern Baptist Theological Seminary, 23 years of adjunct teaching at McAfee School of Theology, lectureships at a number of schools, and pastoring three churches. From 1976–2010 I had the joy of working with the Baptist World Alliance.

When you say yes to God, just get ready for wherever the ride takes you!

Emmanuel McCall is the pastor of First Baptist Church in East Point, Ga. He has served on the faculties of McAfee School of Theology at Mercer University, Candler School of Theology at Emory University, and Southern Baptist Theological Seminary. From 1968–1991 he served on the staff of the Southern Baptist Home Mission Board. Former hobbies included golf, fishing, and photography. Married for 61 years, he is the father of two children and grandfather of four.

Home by Another Way

Emily Hull McGee

"If you could see the journey whole," Jan Richardson says, "you might never undertake it, might never dare the first step that propels you from the place you have known toward the place you know not."

Here I sit, a dozen years out from the first step of the journey I now know to be a calling. What comes clearly into mind is not the memory of a lightning strike or flash of realization, that one clear juncture to pinpoint in which the swing of one's life changed in an instant. Much like my experience of coming to faith and calling Christ my own, my experience of God's calling for ministry unfolded in a collection of moments—flashes in what felt at the time like a dizzying jumble of unrelated experiences, yearnings, convictions, and griefs—but with distance and time with which to draw meaning, those moments look now like the journey of discovery and vocation. God's calling on my life was a dawning.

Perhaps it's appropriate that I write this reflection during Epiphany, the season of the church year when Christians seek to understand the unfolding of God's revelation in Jesus. Epiphany illuminates for us the identity of Jesus as Son and Savior, Liberator and Rescuer, and in his unfolding identity we find our own. In his I found my own, spreading into a call to God's work of love. It announced itself like a rising sun into the dark: first with the slightest slivers of dawn, then a growing awakening of the created world, all coming alive by the Light that shines into the darkness, and finally bursting over the horizon in fiery flame.

My sense of call simply cannot be separated from the context in which it came. I am a preacher's kid, now a third-generation Baptist pastor who has stepped into the well-worn path by the great cloud of witnesses gone ahead of me, the best of whom I call Granddaddy, Aunt, Mom, and Dad. In the churches of my adolescence—the rural parish next to a pig farm in Shelby County, Ky.; the new church plant in suburban Charlotte, N.C.; the charming county seat congregation in small-town Laurens, S.C.; the urban church in the center of downtown Knoxville, Tenn.—our family of four rooted our lives within the church.

My dad served each of these churches as pastor, his time among them filled with his steady wisdom for communal life, strategic mind for organizational transformation, and big heart for God's good news. As "laborers together with God," my parents' north star vision for shared ministry and marriage enabled my mom's vast gifts for ministry and unparalleled capacity to love people with the boldness of God to come to life in all forms during these years. While her role varied along the way—ministries of music, youth, children, seniors all saw her flourishing—she modeled for me the very best of what a minister should be.

My younger brother Andrew and I were folded into these congregational villages, raised up from the cradle roll by Sunday School teachers, RA and GA leaders, Bible drill coaches, missions educators, choir directors, and volunteers who loved God and loved God's church. Our experience of faith took root in colorful measure: biblical characters cheerfully arranged on felt boards in Sunday School, snack times of red Kool-Aid and flower-shaped shortbread cookies on Wednesday nights, outdoor hymn sings fueled by funeral home fans and homemade ice cream, musicals of grand scope that gave us space to celebrate life, and youth camps and trips that reminded us of who and whose we were.

Even as my questions about God continued to increase as I grew older, I honestly never felt anything but genuine love in the church, my particular place in the shape of our common life together secure and celebrated. So complete was my affirmation as a young Christian girl—enhanced, in part I'm sure, due to members' love for my minister parents—that it never occurred to me that this wasn't normal for any child of the church. That is, until God beckoned me down a different road.

My long love of music-making led me to pursue back-to-back music degrees in vocal performance—a bachelor's at Furman University in Greenville, S.C., and then a master's at Northwestern University in Chicago. In both of these seasons of my life, but especially the latter, I began to hear a different story about the church from the dear friends I made along the way. They were artists and creatives, vibrant members of the LGBTQ community, irreverent and cynical, loyal and fun. And gratefully, they loved me well. Bound together by a common experience in a particular season of life, we became a family.

As we grew together, I learned that every one of these friends had grown up in the Christian church and, without fail, every one of them save for a couple had walked away from it. Their church stories were of indifference and suffering, neglect and abuse, simply because of who they were. It's not that my friends didn't want to talk about God or faith—quite the opposite. They seemed hungry for God and God's long story of justice and reconciliation. They wanted to reckon with Scripture, dig into the problem of evil, and imagine God's dream for this world. We talked about faith often, but we did so lavishly, loudly, safely *outside* the church, certainly not within it.

Reconciling this deep chasm between the loving churches of my experience and the rejecting churches of my friends' experience utterly transformed me. I saw clearly the point of tension between deprivation and flourishing, between exclusion and embrace. It burdened me and burned within me. "Someone should do something about this!" I remember thinking. And right there for me, the first hints of light, of revelation, of calling began to streak for me across the darkened sky of my life.

With these moments were others. There was the late-night phone call to Mom and Dad, made when driving home from an audition. My words were as jumbled and disjointed as my unexpected tears, the latter articulating for me what I couldn't yet express—that the musical dream I had for my life was dimming. I loved the creation of music: the rapturous beauty and hope it captured in the imagination of the listener, the community of artists with whom I could share it, and the process of honing the craft. I did not, however, love the business of music: the never-ending, uncertain cycle of audition circuits and hypercritical judges, sharp competition that stacked a huge supply of great young singers in an acutely-narrowing demand, random jobs taken simply to support the singing habit.

There were the hours spent watching news coverage of Hurricane Katrina shortly after it made landfall, weeping in horror at my desk as I sat hopelessly disconnected from such real human suffering. My day job was as an insurance company receptionist, nestled high and safe on the 18th floor of a downtown Chicago high-rise a block from the Sears Tower. I watched and wondered, "What in the world am I even *doing* here?!"

There were other wonderings-out-loud with parents and friends, a growing curiosity to imagine what the shape of my life could look like if not singing, to—despite my surprise—maybe think about seminary. My folks met and fell in love at Southern Baptist Theological Seminary in Louisville, Ky., decades ago, and throughout my life they spoke of those years as some of their best. In my wonderings I allowed myself to articulate a truth I think I'd known for years but just never said out loud: *What if I should go to seminary too?*

There was that one snowy and unforgettable afternoon spent at the coffeeshop near my apartment, finally writing my admissions essays for divinity school. Somehow, simply the prompt itself—to put words to these wonderings—contained a spark of the Spirit's ember that allowed my heart to grow strangely warmed. Somehow, the star now shone aways overhead, unmistakable, beckoning me to summon the courage to take the first step.

There were the visits to divinity schools, chances to articulate whatever this thing was that was causing me to be there. (In still such an uncertain state, did I dare start using the word "call"?) Those visits included: lunches with students in whom I heard reflections of my own story; conversations with faculty, especially those now immortalized in my communion of saints—Doctors Bill Leonard, Frank Tupper, Diane Lipsett, Jill Crainshaw, and James Dunn; worship that brought me to my knees with its earthy, incarnational truth. There was a powerful dawning upon me that were I to leave singing for seminary, were I to move from Chicago to Winston-Salem, were I to step away from the road less traveled to join a familiar, familial path, it would be a journey leading me home … but for me, now, a journey home by another way.

I wish I could say such a rising epiphany of calling crowded out my fears of such a transition and made me more trusting, softer, and suppler for God to take and use for the work of love in the world. But even as God's persistent call became louder, if not yet clearer with every passing day I spent at Wake Forest University School of Divinity, I still pressed stubbornly against the thought of parish ministry.

I remember my defiant announcement to my family: "Now, just because I'm going to divinity school does *not* mean I'm going to work in a church, and it definitely does not mean I'm going to become a minister! I'm not! I mean it! Really!" ("The lady doth protest too much, methinks!")

I remember the time my Granddaddy Bill, hot with a rare flash of anger, responded correctively to a comment I made, flippantly and with privilege I had yet to see or understand. I didn't want to spend the rest of my life arguing with Baptists about women in ministry, I had declared, so I'd just as soon go be a Methodist instead. A decade later, his words humble me still.

I remember talking with my parents and my Aunt Susan, trying to sort out how to fashion a real job in ministry from the unformed clay I held: a love for God and neighbor, a renewed hopefulness about God's church, a handful of fierce convictions, a tug toward people in a similar life stage and outlook, and an imperfect-yet-hopeful vessel.

And I remember the surge of resurrecting boldness I saw among the people of Highland Baptist Church in Louisville, a shared place to claim honestly together a calling that carried me to my first job out of seminary there as minister to young adults.

Since that extended season, God's calling on my life has shifted and stirred, sometimes flooding my life with clarity and conviction, other times illuminating paths I would never have taken on my own. "Call it one of the mercies of the road," Jan Richardson writes, "that we see it only by stages as it comes into our keeping, step by single step." But when I remember that first light of calling, I give thanks for the God who calls and keeps, the God who beckoned me to follow the star at its rising, the God who comes as the Light of the World.

Emily Hull McGee is the pastor of First Baptist Church on Fifth in Winston-Salem, N.C. She is the proud daughter of David and Jane Hull, both pastors and leaders in their Georgia home and beyond. Emily is married to Josh and is mom to Liam, Annabelle, and Silas.

Discovering My Call

Barrett Owen

My dad, brothers, and I raced a mile to the end of the road. It did not dawn on me early enough, but the downside to running a mile away from home is, eventually, you have to run back. My brothers raced with ease into the second mile. My dad and I walked it.

On that walk I remember asking him, "Where is God? We talk about him being up in the sky, but we've been up. We've been to the moon. Did we pass heaven? How high is up?" These questions (and others like it) plagued my nine-year-old mind.

My dad tried to explain spiritual dimensions to me, but I struggled to conceptualize it. Despite my ignorance, I remember how alive I felt even in the asking of the questions. It did not matter if I completely understood; I was mesmerized just by the thought. I can still feel that memory's energy and how my soul was embarking on a journey toward divine mystery.

Fast forward to middle school. I attended Passport summer camp at Stetson University in central Florida. My Bible study leader asked me one morning to lead the prayer that night in worship. I proudly, but fearfully, said yes.

My heart still races when I think about the pressure I felt in the hours leading up to worship. I had been asked to stand before hundreds of my peers to deliver a prayer to God. What would I even say? I knew I needed to prepare.

During free time early that afternoon I got out my notebook and sat under a tree. But I had nothing. After a few uncomfortable seconds I took a silent walk through the athletic fields in an attempt to clear my head. It did not work. I still had nothing. Two hours went by and I had nothing. Dinner finished and I had nothing. We lined up for worship and I had nothing. We finished the opening worship set! I had nothing. I was ushered backstage for the second music set, and still I had nothing.

The lights went dark. The music stopped. A single spotlight hit the stage. It was my turn. I had nothing prepared. I slowly walked to the mic and fearfully yet boldly said, "Pray with me."

I cannot explain what happened next. I started to speak, but I do not know what I said. I probably quoted a 1995 contemporary Christian song about being a sanctuary or lighting fires in my soul, but whatever it was, I have no memory of it.

What I do remember is there was also a moment during the prayer when I opened my eyes and thought, "This is not me talking. I have no idea what's happening. This is awesome. I love this."

My mom happened to be chaperoning that trip. After my prayer she hugged me and said, "That was beautiful, Barrett." I knew I had experienced something real. I can still feel the energy of that memory and how my soul continued on its journey toward divine mystery.

Fast forward to high school. Each year we attended the Senior Beta Club's state convention at Opryland Hotel in Nashville, Tenn. Thousands of high schoolers came together for a weekend of competition and learning.

During my junior year I ran for state president. This meant I had to give a two-minute speech at the opening convocation and then my club had to perform a one-minute skit featuring our campaign slogan.

I was ushered onstage with my notecards in hand. I was fifth out of about seven to speak. Each person before me went onstage right to the podium, read her/his speech, and felt the weight of speaking in front of 5,000 people.

After the fourth speaker finished I was brought the microphone. It was my turn. I put my notecards in my jacket pocket and thought, "I got this." I walked center stage, passed by the podium, stood firm, stared out into a room of 5,000 people, and I spoke. I was nervous but confident. My mind cleared, and the words flowed. I delivered my speech just like I rehearsed in the mirror.

Afterwards, I told my friends, "I don't know what I will do with my life, but I know it will include this." I loved it. The rush, the pressure, the peace, it was intoxicating. I did not win, but what I took away from that moment I still carry today. My soul continued on its journey toward divine mystery.

Fast forward to college. I applied to be the pastor at youth summer camps, and I was selected. At 20 years old I traveled for 11 weeks to five states with a team of 14, preaching twice a day, five days a week to introduce kids to the stories and nature of Jesus.

To put it mildly, I struggled. More sermons than not were bad. I spoke too fast. I spoke too long. I did not really know how to speak in a way that invited listeners into the stories of Jesus, nor did I know how to help pull them out of the stories in order to make applications. I feel sorry for the churches that watched me struggle, but despite my failings, I loved it.

I loved the stage. I loved the stories of Scripture. I loved Jesus in a seismic way that captured my soul's attention. I knew this was my calling, but I needed more training, so in college I majored in Christian leadership and minored in biblical studies.

I took a church job at age 21 and went to seminary at 22. I was hired by a small, rural church as a co-pastor and preached every week at 23. Every one of these stages intensified my calling and fueled my soul to continue on its journey toward divine mystery.

It propelled me to attain an advanced degree in homiletics and to work and teach at my seminary while preaching weekly as a bi-vocational pastor. In all of these roles my soul kept unfolding toward divine mystery, and I loved it. It made me feel alive.

I came to understand calling as what makes us feel alive while offering opportunities to lean toward (and help others experience) divine mystery. It may hit us seismically or slowly, but as it unfolds, our soul moves toward divine mystery.

Years ago I accepted a call to be the pastor of First Baptist Church in Waynesboro, Va. My family moved nine hours north from Atlanta to a community we had visited only once. During the call weekend the church held a question-and-answer session for anyone and everyone to come and meet my family and ask me questions.

I remember being asked how I understand faith and calling. In a flash, some of these memories flooded my mind and I remembered an old quote from Rudolf Otto: "Faith is awe in the face of mystery."

I shared this quote and said, "My calling is to invite people through the stories of Scripture to encounter God by helping them see and experience awe in the face of mystery." Even today I still feel called to help others experience awe in the face of mystery, to see God with a sense of wonder and hope, to believe that which comes to us is from the Great Unknown and is for us and from a good God.

This is my calling, and I feel it manifesting with every sermon in the pulpit, every conversation with families, every mission trip with youth, every Wednesday night meal, and every pastoral visit. I want to help others experience awe in the face of mystery.

But there is something new I am learning.

We had a bad ice storm in Waynesboro. Trees all over the city collapsed, schools were closed, and our yard suffered quite a bit of damage. It happened right before Thanksgiving one year when my family and I left town for a week.

Upon returning, a church member called, knowing I had hours of work ahead of me in my yard. He asked if it would be ok if he sawed down my fallen trees. I did not know what more to say other than, "My gosh. That would be amazing." He thanked me for all I do for him and said he wanted to do something only he could do for me.

Here is something new I am learning about calling: It is not just about me and my experiences. It is not just about my prayers or my sermons or my speeches or my jobs. It is about those to a degree, but it is also about how others engage their calling and the way in which they give of their time and their personhood and their life to God. Our callings are interwoven encounters that awaken our souls to a journey that moves the world toward divine mystery. Whatever that looks like for you is part of your calling.

Barrett Owen is the senior pastor of First Baptist Church in Waynesboro, Va. He and his wife, Noelle, love living in the Shenandoah Valley and serving the community together with their two children, Henry and Georgia.

Called from the Very "First"

Bill Owen

It was the "first" paper I would ever write, at least the first one required of me. In the first grade of Graceland Elementary School in Memphis, Tenn., my teacher assigned the title, "What I Want to Be When I Grow Up." In no more than two sentences I finished and then illustrated it with an ever-so-humble stick drawing. There I stood, preaching atop a raised box.

I realize the initial impulse was to be like my father, a pastor and preacher. After all, I am the firstborn. Much later I would recognize this question as the same one that hounded me through adulthood, "Is the life I am living the same as the life that wants to live in me?" Or, "Is this the life that God has called me to live?"

I was born in Nashville while my father, married and fresh out of military service in the Korean War, was enrolled at Belmont College (now Belmont University) in Nashville. As newlyweds, Mom and Dad attended Woodmont Baptist Church. It was there in a nursery crib that my newborn photo appeared on the front cover of the *Home Life* magazine of the Baptist Sunday School Board. As I remember it, the church called us "bed babies."

I was born in the church.

During those Belmont days Dad became the pastor of a church in Guthrie, Ky. We spent our weekends there. On one particular weekend my dad went ahead of my mom and me. So, joined by Aunt Dot, my mother's sister, we struck out for Guthrie to join Dad and the church at the weekend revival. On the way we had an automobile accident. As the story goes, I was thrown from the car, landing in a bed of glass unharmed. The apocryphal version has it that I never awakened from sleep. We made it to the revival, where, perhaps, I continued to sleep.

Following graduation from Belmont, we moved to New Orleans where my father attended seminary and served as the student pastor of a little church down in the bayou, a place called Homa, La. I remember throwing my first rocks into the river waters there.

I was in the church from the very beginning.

My earliest memories issue from the church and from Dad's college and seminary days. Listening to one's life, if I hear Parker Palmer correctly (*Let Your Life Speak*), is the goal. All along the way I have listened as best I can, trying to understand my life and what it is to be about.

The church was my first seminary experience.

"Seminary" means literally "seed bed." The church is meant to be the "nursery" where boys and girls are to be cultivated. It is in the church that seeds are planted that will bear good fruit—God willing—in the future.

I was born in the church.

I was planted in the church by a mother and father who loved me. Our friends, the people whom we did life with, were in the church. I never knew any different.

I remember one particular family, the Simpsons, who lived across the street from us in Memphis on Windcrest Road. As an adult now, I can see the connection between my parents and these neighbors. They were church members, and they also were from Louisiana. Since Mom and Dad had spent their early married life together in New Orleans during seminary, there was love for all things Cajun. Red beans and rice, gumbo, and boiled shrimp made up a great percentage of Mom's favorite dishes to prepare. After all, we had spent those seminary years in a little bayou church.

I cannot count how many Friday or Saturday evenings we would gather around a large kitchen table sharing a meal with the Simpsons—boiled shrimp in particular, freshly delivered from Louisiana. Those early memories of table fellowship, watching friends and neighbors laugh and eat, were like church to me. The people from church were neighbors my family loved. As a young boy, I knew in my deepest parts this was good—not just the shrimp, but the life shared.

"Call" in its simplest form is a voice to be heard. This is what I know to be true in my experience. It would be my life's current. I listened as best I knew to parents who loved me and church people who embraced me.

Dad's pastoral ministry took us from Memphis to two more churches in Middle Tennessee during my school years. At each step, church league baseball coaches, Bible teachers, and Royal Ambassador leaders would link arms with my parents as moral influencers and character builders.

In the middle of my sophomore year, during the Christmas holiday break, my father accepted a call to another church. Initially, I was none too happy about it. High school football had taken on great significance. Marshall County High had gone to the Tennessee state semifinal game. I loved being on a successful team. Besides, DeKalb County, where we would move, had never sniffed anything near that level of accomplishment.

So, it was hard for me to see the wisdom of such a move. The church we would go to and the house we would live in were smaller than what we had known. And the football team, good grief, had not had a winning season in 10 years!

However, I'll never forget the first day of spring football practice. The head football coach, Wayne Cantrell, introduced himself to me and asked, "Bill, what position do you play?"

I'm still not sure how to describe what I heard him say, much less how I summoned the strength to answer as I did that day, other than it was a response that came from deep down, from my core. It had been percolating there all along. Images from my first days on the middle school football field as a Connelly Jet flashed before me. I had always wanted to play quarterback, to lead the team, to call the plays, to encourage everyone around me to be and give their best.

So, when Coach Cantrell asked, I answered the voice that I had heard like this: "I play quarterback."

And so, though I never had, I did. Thanks to good coaching and a talented team, we ran off two consecutive winning seasons. Space doesn't allow for all the life and leadership lessons I learned during those critical years, but suffice it to say I am thankful for every voice that spoke into those life experiences.

The takeaway from those "good ole days" was simple. I had always known that "we" could do much more than "I," and so those lessons on the playing field were priceless. They translated into team-building skills such as culture-building, establishing trust and rapport among others, and overcoming challenges that always come. The call to come alongside people, joining hand and heart in pursuit of a common goal, has always been the certain and clear sound to me.

"Too short, too slow" was not the recipe for a future as a football player. That was obvious. But just as apparent was the connection to my life in the church. I had sensed this same kind of purpose and passion in my father's preaching, the dedication and commitment in my mother's prayers. Perhaps, even in elementary school, that was calling me to dream about what I wanted to be when I grew up.

The church in Alexandria, Tenn., would be the place I preached my first sermon, was "licensed" to preach, and then was ordained to pastoral ministry. More than one of the "elders" in that small-town church would encourage me to lean in to my giftedness. Every whisper of affirmation and hug of acceptance meant the world to me. I am thankful to each person who supported me. From Alexandria I went to Belmont College, where I majored in religion, met lifelong friends, sat among professors and students—with each one contributing to the flow of my life's current.

Were it not for my parents' shared faith and commitment to these local communities of faith, I don't think I would have ever listened to, much less heard, the call to ministry. There's no doubt from where I stand that this current of life was always moving beneath the surface. God was always calling from within and without these experiences and relationships.

I believe pastoral ministry, particularly as vocation, is something God does—not that I always knew it at the time, but God did, in and always through my life's story. For me, my ministry has come through family, the church, coaches, teachers, and life experiences before anything else.

Will Willimon reminds us that church leaders come both from the "bottom up"—the ranks of those whom the community chooses to lead—and from the "top down," as gifts of a gracious God who does not leave the church without the guidance it needs to fulfill its mission (*Calling and Character*, pp. 15-16). That rings true with my experience.

Pastoral ministry has taken me to three churches, the first as a student at Belmont. Dry Creek Baptist Church in Dowelltown, Tenn., loved me as a young, single student. My wife, Cindy, and I then served Immanuel Baptist Church in Shepherdsville, Ky., while I was studying at Southern Baptist Theological Seminary in Louisville. Then we served for 32 years at Mt. Carmel Baptist Church of Cross Plains, Tenn. I have been asked more than once why I stayed in one church so long. I am not sure how to answer that other than I never sensed God's call to go elsewhere. Some asked, others encouraged; but I never really felt compelled to do so.

Frederick Buechner reminds us that true Christianity finds itself in the flesh and blood of real life, in our life stories. As a pastor in the same community for more than three decades, I felt the joy of what Buechner writes. My family and I built a life within a particular community. We were accountable to them. We laughed and cried, played and worked, worshiped and served, celebrated and mourned together. We enjoyed the simple things and worked our way through challenges along the way. We came alongside one another as friends and neighbors. At our best, we were Christ to one another.

As a congregational coach with the Center for Healthy Churches, I'm finding the same possibilities now working alongside local congregations, church leadership teams, and ministry staffs. It is life-giving.

My calling is something that God did in and through my family, the churches we served and worshipped in. If there is any significance in my story, it is that God has continued calling me all through my life, and I am prone to listen for and to his voice. I am thankful to parents who taught me to do so, to friends and colleagues who coached me along the way, and most of all to a current that continually flowed, from opportunity to opportunity, to and from deep within.

Bill Owen retired after serving for 32 years as the senior pastor at Mt. Carmel Baptist Church in Cross Plains, Tenn. He now serves as a congregational and leadership coach with the Center for Healthy Churches, and as an adjunct professor at Belmont University in Nashville. Bill also enjoys interim pastoral leadership and preaching.

There and Back Again

Brandon Owen

Born in Louisville during my dad's years at Southern Baptist Theological Seminary in Louisville, Ky., we moved to middle Tennessee when I was two to a very small town north of Nashville called Cross Plains. My parents still live there. Dad was the pastor of Mt. Carmel Baptist Church for more than 30 years, and Mom was a special education teacher in my high school. The oldest of three boys, to say we had a wonderful childhood experience would be underselling it. How many ministers' kids get to see their minister parent/pastor at the same address for 30-plus years?

My brothers and I grew to love the church. My younger brother, Barrett, and I are ordained as ministers, and Blake is ordained as a deacon. We still love the church. I never felt pressure to love the church, though. I don't even remember thinking much about the church being a significant source of our family's livelihood. From a young age I remember feeling a part of the church, even before my baptism. I experienced Mt. Carmel as a healthy place, a place where I learned the stories of our faith and worshiped with God's people.

I did well in school and was generally liked by my peers. In retrospect, I was a bit more self-righteous than I wish I had been. It certainly cost me some friendships. But I remember high school fondly. I learned I had some giftedness in being able to get along with people. More importantly, I learned I had a strong desire to know people. Looking back, I can see now that I was inclined at a young age to be a pastor.

Sports were, and still are, a big part of my life. I was a decent athlete with an above-average set shot. High school basketball was a good experience, and I had some opportunities to play Division 3 college ball. But those schools didn't give athletic scholarships, so to attend would be pricy.

My parents met at Belmont University in Nashville, so we had always been Belmont fans. I had grown up going to summer camps and attending home games there. So, when I sat down with Coach Byrd during the summer before I began school there, he hit me with some hard truth: I was not really good enough to contribute as a walk-on player. But if I would like to be the team manager, he would pay for the balance of my tuition, room, and board. I had enough sense as an 18-year-old to know that was a good deal for me and my family.

Being a part of that basketball program has been a significant part of my journey. I am still close with Coach Byrd and many others at and from Belmont. It is where I met Betty Wiseman, the senior women's administrator and former women's basketball coach. Her heart was for world evangelism as she used the game of basketball to take many of us all over the world to tell people about Jesus. Those short-term trips taught me that I both enjoyed and was gifted at sharing my faith. It also expanded my southern small-town worldview.

I began college intent upon plugging into a church. I attended Brentwood Baptist first. The pastor there, Mike Glenn, is a gifted communicator. Then I attended First Baptist Nashville because Frank Lewis, the new pastor, was in a small group of pastors with my dad. Dad had told me how much he liked Frank. I also attended a Tuesday night worship gathering for college students led, in part, by the student minister at First Baptist. I was drawn to him, and he empowered me. He made me believe I had something to offer the church by working with students. I will be forever grateful for Jeff Simmons speaking into my life in such a way. So, I plugged in at First Baptist and did not leave for 20 years.

I never gravitated over to the School of Religion at Belmont. I really wish I had, but I was probably bent on not following in my father's path exactly, so I majored in business and focused on learning the game of basketball. I either wanted to be a college coach or a missionary. I had a desire to be like Coach Byrd or Betty. But I knew I wanted to work with people. Coaching was particularly intriguing to me because I recognized the opportunity it afforded to be such a huge part of a young man's formation while having a blast competing. So, I entered graduate school and stayed on with the basketball program for two more years with the hopes of getting onto a collegiate staff somewhere.

During this time, I was still serving the youth group at First Baptist. As we were preparing for the summer months of 2002, I met Lesley Ann Howell. Sixteen months later we were married. With her job as a nurse at Vanderbilt University, my plans to go coach basketball at an obscure school in an obscure town went away. Not long thereafter, I finished grad school and found myself in a meeting with the headmaster of a local Christian high school, Brentwood Academy. I had no teaching license or experience outside of discipleship training. But the job to teach the school's senior year Bible class had opened up. And the basketball coach wanted me, so I was hired. For the next seven years I was effectively a youth minister and basketball coach. And I loved every minute of it.

Brentwood Academy has a policy of paying 100 percent of its faculty's continuing education. As I continued to grow as a teacher, I began to understand how much I loved teaching my Bible class. So, I enrolled in seminary at Hazelip School of Theology in Nashville. It was during this time that I was becoming more aware of some of the public relations problems Christians were having—intolerant, narrow-minded, etc. I remember feeling as if some of the fundamentalism that my dad had done a good job of helping us keep at an arm's distance was too prevalent in our evangelical circles. And such fundamentalism was hurting our ability to effectively share the love of Jesus. Instead of pulling away from the church, I felt a distinct pull further in. For the first time in my life I felt like the Spirit was giving me some specific direction. It was as if God were saying, "Don't be a nay-sayer, Brandon; go work within the church."

It was around this time that First Baptist was going through another youth pastor exodus. Since Jeff Simmons had left to plant a church in 2003, no youth pastor had stayed for more than two years. So, in December of 2010, Frank Lewis and I sat down over eggs and had a conversation that would change our lives. Four months later I left a job I loved and was getting pretty good at for a job I hoped I would be good at. I stopped coaching and became the student minister at First Baptist Nashville. At the time Lesley Ann and I were expecting our second child. So, we had my work at Brentwood Academy, Lesley Ann's work at Vanderbilt, our work as volunteer leaders at First Baptist, and our growing home life. In a strange way, going into vocational ministry simplified our life.

After three years of student ministry and a third child, I began to feel the pinch of those summer months on my family. It was around that time that we were, as a church staff, praying through adding a contemporary worship service that would, at least some weeks, require a preacher other than Frank Lewis. I had filled in for Frank a few times at that point, and I knew that I enjoyed preaching. But preaching weekly was a different animal, and as we got further into the planning it became clear that this role was going to require a weekly preacher. What began as an experiment and quite a few very rough sermons has become the greatest joy of my professional life. I love preparing and delivering sermons. I am so grateful First Baptist gave me the opportunity to preach regularly.

My journey has come full circle. I am now the pastor of a church in Nashville that has merged with Brentwood Baptist Church in association with Brentwood's Middle Tennessee Initiative. Mike Glenn is in his 27th year as Brentwood's pastor, and I will serve on a team of pastors led by him. Bill Wilson, director of the Center for Healthy Churches, calls my new role "a lead pastor job with half of the headaches." I am excited about this new opportunity. I love the church. I believe it is God's plan for God's people. I am eager to continue leaning into what it looks like to partner with God's mission in the world to bring about God's Kingdom on earth as it is in heaven.

While I have not experienced God explicitly directing my steps along my journey, as I look back, I can see the signposts that helped me along the way. I have been helped and loved immensely as I have navigated the maze of my pastoral call. As a pastor, I see the importance of being a good shepherd and a good preacher. But I also see the importance of being an equipper. I have been equipped by so many, and I want to do that for others by helping them to partner with God in God's mission in the world. I have come to understand that the question before me is not what kind of mission God has for me in the world. Rather, the question is what kind of me God wants for God's mission. My call is to help others understand the same.

Brandon Owen is the teaching pastor at Harpeth Heights Baptist Church in Nashville, Tenn. Brandon and Lesley Ann have been married for 15 years and have four children: Howell, Elliott, Louis, and Hattie. A graduate of Belmont University and Central Baptist Theological Seminary, Brandon enjoys running, playing golf, and spending time with his family and friends.

Dawnings

Julie Pennington-Russell

When I was a little girl I would sometimes crawl into my father's lap after supper. Sitting under our screened-in carport with his arms around me on those evenings, my face pressed into the fabric of his shirt, I would close my eyes and inhale. The faint memory of beer mingled with Old Spice and tobacco is still pleasant to me, even after all this time. On such evenings, as Dad and I rocked back and forth, it was not unusual to hear from inside the house my mother singing the words to some old gospel hymn: "Every day with Jesus is sweeter than the day before. Every day with Jesus . . . I love him more and more."

I grew up in a home marked by a kind of spiritual duality that had a profound and lasting effect on me. My mother, Barbara, who professed her faith at the age of 21 after an encounter with two Southern Baptist door-to-door evangelists, is a fundamentalist Christian who loves nothing more than delving deep into the Word of God. At the other end of the spiritual spectrum was my father, Ron, who was baptized as a boy at the 35th Avenue Baptist Church in Birmingham, Ala. He left church about the time he enlisted in the U.S. Air Force at the age of 20 and remained at arm's length from God for the next 45 years, until his death in 1999.

As a child, I felt drawn to the rhythms of faith to which my mother moved. I also loved the earthy, funny, off-color ways of my father. My mother taught me by example that following Christ means plunging all the way in, not dabbling one's toes at the edge of the water. At the same time, my father, who had a fondness for just about every vice on the Baptist "Thou Shalt Not" list, was also the kindest, humblest, most generous person I knew. This was a signal to me from childhood that the lines we sometimes draw and the labels we assign—good/bad, saint/reprobate, saved/unsaved—never tell the whole story about any person.

Mom imparted to me her love of Jesus. Dad taught me not to muck up my faith by confusing it with religion. Best of all, my family-of-origin experience gave me the gift of feeling equally at home with people of significant faith and people of little or no faith. I relate to both, love being with both, and love offering the gospel in the midst of both.

I made my public profession of faith when I was nine and my father was stationed at McCoy Air Force Base in Orlando, Fla. At the Sky Lake Baptist Church I'd been hearing the stories and singing the songs about Jesus, and I knew I wanted to give my life to Christ. Of course, I didn't fully understand what I was committing to, or what it meant to be a Christ-follower in the world, but that didn't matter. I've heard faith described as "giving all of yourself you can to all of the Christ you know." That still sounds about right to me, and that's pretty much what I did when I knelt beside my bed one summer evening in 1969.

That night, after confessing to God all the sins I could think of and asking Jesus to come into my life, I got off my knees and went into the living room to share with my family the happy news of my salvation. Dad was on a tour of duty in Vietnam, but my mother and grandmothers were there, watching a television show. They turned the volume down when I asked them to, but suddenly I felt self-conscious and only managed to sputter, "Well, I guess I'm saved." They celebrated with me for a few moments, then cranked the TV back up. That was it. My conversion is forever linked in my mind to the theme song from *Mission: Impossible*.

An early piece of my own story has to do with God's providence at work, even before I was alive. In 1956, four years before I was born, it became apparent to my father that he would not be able to go to college because he needed to work to help support his widowed mother and younger sister. Dad's decision to enlist in the Air Force rearranged the trajectory of my life because it removed my family from Alabama forever.

My parents always spoke fondly to me of growing up in Alabama, but Birmingham in the 1960s was in many ways a broken city. And so, while my cousins were growing up in a place of fire hoses and church bombings and ubiquitous "White Only" and "Colored Only" signs, my brother and I were living out in California in military housing with our neighbors, the Washingtons, who were African American; the Schwartzes, who were Jewish; and the Awohis, who were Pacific Islander. Their children were our everyday playmates. Such diversity shaped my life in important ways. What's more, at that time in California, the women's liberation movement was in full swing. In those days Helen Reddy was singing, "I am woman, hear me roar." In my young heart a seed was planted, and I concluded: "I can be anything God wants me to be."

The years we spent in the San Joaquin Valley of California when I was in junior high and high school were some of the most formative of my life. My happy memories of those days would draw me back to the West Coast years later, when I decided to enter seminary. I realize now that God somehow took a part of my father's shattered dream of attending college and fashioned from those broken pieces a path for me that still feels beautiful beneath my feet.

I need to admit upfront that my discernment process before entering seminary could not have been more half-baked. My father had retired from the Air Force, and we were living again in Orlando. I was about to graduate from the University of Central Florida and the only thing in life I was sure of was that I *didn't* want to be a speech pathologist, which I'd just spent four years learning how to be. I also belonged to a large Southern Baptist church in Orlando and was very active there. Embedded in the culture of the college group was a peculiar assumption that following Christ in earnest automatically meant going to seminary. It was just the "spiritual" thing to do. No particular call? No problem. Just go to seminary and see if you get one.

And so, six months after my college graduation, with no idea where it would lead and without any clear sense of being "called" to some particular ministry (in fact, as a young woman from a fundamentalist background, the only thing I did know was that I certainly wasn't called to be a pastor), I climbed on a plane in Orlando with $11 in my pocket and an acceptance letter from Golden Gate Baptist Theological Seminary, just north of San Francisco.

Worst vocational discernment story ever.

But in hindsight that experience taught me that God is able to take even half-baked motives, convoluted theology, and a general lack of maturity and craft from these a surprising recipe for a call.

I arrived at seminary as thoroughly Southern Baptist as I could be. Every morning during my first semester I got up an hour early and headed to the little prayer room at the end of my dormitory hallway. There I would get on my knees and pray for all the poor, misguided women in my classes who thought God was calling them to be pastors.

But over time, God began to open up some sky over my faith and I began to see God and faith and the Bible and the church—as well as myself—through new eyes. In seminary the neat little systems of faith I'd been handed as a child began to give way to a faith that was broader and deeper and more mysterious than I'd experienced before.

It was also during seminary that I met a California-born, Hawaii-raised free spirit named Tim Russell who, after 30 years of marriage, continues to be the best life partner for me imaginable. Tim's enthusiastic support of my calling and his ready willingness to move around the country as the Spirit has led us to different congregations has been, and is, pure gift.

A series of pivotal moments occurred for me while in San Francisco. As I mentioned earlier, I began seminary with very little sense of calling except for the persuasion that women couldn't and shouldn't be pastors. But one chilly Sunday morning in the spring of 1983, I visited a small, two-story wooden church located on a main thoroughfare in San Francisco, two blocks from Golden Gate Park. From the moment I walked through the door at Nineteenth Avenue Baptist Church, I knew there was something beautiful and particularly God-connected about this community. The spirit of life and joy among this congregation of about 100 was palpable. As it turned out, they needed a music minister and I had some modest musical skills. When the pastor and congregation invited me to lead the music, I needed some time to discern: "Is this a door God is opening?" As a former fundamentalist Christian, asking and answering that question required me to trust in the God who says, "Look, I'm doing something new!" I said yes.

When I graduated from seminary two years later the congregation asked, "Will you become our associate pastor?" More discernment: "God, do you mean for me to walk through this door?" Again, I perceived a divine yes, just as I would discern seven years later, when that same community asked me to be their pastor. Over a period of 14 years at Nineteenth Avenue I served in three different ministerial roles. At each juncture, however, I wrestled with God as I listened for hints of guidance and grace.

My experience of call over the past 35 years rarely has come with trumpets and bright lights. In truth, God's calling mostly has dawned on me by inches and hunches and best-guesses and has seemed less like barreling down a wide, well-marked freeway and more like walking a labyrinth at night, holding a birthday candle. Along the way I've learned how to be less nervous about "getting my call right." After all, the Bible itself is surprisingly "unanxious" about the "what" and is more concerned with the "Who." As I see it, my first calling is to bind myself to God; to affix my heart to Christ. In doing that, I find enormous freedom to do what I do best and to do what I love best. My *first* calling, though, is to belong to the Beloved.

Julie Pennington-Russell is the senior pastor of the First Baptist Church of the City of Washington, D.C. She and her husband, Tim, are the parents of two young adult children, Taylor and Lucy.

There Is Power in Our Stories

Aurelia Davila Pratt

The rows of stuffed bears are staring back at me from the brown, shag carpet of my childhood bedroom. There are a few Care Bears, along with two esteemed guests: a thick, old, white bear called Snow Joe and a smaller, light brown bear named Honey Joe. I take out my rosary and the little white book containing the order of the Mass, which I received at my first communion. I take out the plate and cup I swiped from the kitchen to be used during the Eucharist. Meanwhile, my furry congregants are lined up against the popcorned walls of my bedroom, ready for me to read the liturgy aloud. I begin just as the priest does; just like my little white book says. And after my Mass has ended, I find that the bears seem a bit more holy and the room feels as though it has had an encounter with the divine.

Now I am in the kitchen of the quaint 1,200-square-foot home I grew up in. It is a Sunday evening in December, and I am leaning my head against the wooden paneling. All the lights are out, and we are sitting around the kitchen table as a family. Then, in the same place where we break bread and share life each day, my dad recites a reading. He instructs me to light the candle that is nestled into the Advent wreath, and I eagerly reach toward the pink one. "Not yet," he says. "Light the purple one for now." I strike the match; I light the candle. And while I don't fully grasp its meaning at the time, the pictures of that moment are burned into my memory, and I recall the sense that my heart was ablaze in that ordinary moment turned holy. I knew God was present among us as surely as the linoleum floor was below my swinging legs.

Now I am a freshman in college. I am lying outside late one night, staring at the stars. I am reflecting on all the people I have met so far who have shaped my life so much in a short time. I am thinking about how I'd like to be like them. Many nameless to me now; many only a brush of interaction for a season, and yet their stories shape my story monumentally. I am lying on a blanket. It is not quite big enough, so the moisture from the grass touches my heels. I look up and say, "God, I want to be called, but you have to 'call' me first." And I mutter that paraphrase from Isaiah: "Here am I . . . send me!" (It was years later that I realized in that moment in the grass under the stars, in that ordinary moment turned holy, God had already called me the moment I yearned to follow.)

Ten years later I am in an airport just weeks before my ordination ceremony. My flight delay is delayed—pushed back repeatedly. It is late and I am tired, uncomfortable, and eager to be home. To pass the time, I take out a book by Barbara Brown Taylor. I thought it was a book on preaching, but in it she speaks often of her journey to ordination. She reminisces about one midnight when she asked God what she was supposed to do with her life. Again and again she heard God respond, "Do anything that pleases you, and belong to me." She says, "I decided that it would please me to become a priest and to spend the rest of my life with a community willing to help me figure out what that meant."

Suddenly, in the same moment when I was tired, agitated, and trying my hardest to make as little contact with airport germs as possible—in that ordinary moment turned holy—I found that her words were my words. Her struggle with call and ordination was the same as mine. And her peace was my peace, too, as I realized I would never have to walk any road alone. Whether it had to do with calling, ordination or spiritual growth, I had a community of believers in the church; a great cloud of witnesses by my side, committed to supporting me on the journey. When I finally boarded the plane a little later, I realized I was changed by this revelation. And when the day of my ceremony finally came, my heart was able to hold the sacredness of ordination and what it meant for my life more fully.

Most recently, motherhood revealed the intricate relationship between the mundane and the holy in a new way. Nothing has changed me so much and so quickly the way becoming a mother has. I remember the first few weeks of postpartum, the fog of sleeplessness. I remember the mental, emotional, and spiritual whiplash one can only experience when your life changes drastically. I remember wondering how I would ever find the brain space to write another sermon, much less a good one. And I also remember the moment when I looked up and realized that my writing had changed for the better. The best sermons I have written are on the other side of motherhood. Becoming a mom woke up my heart in a new way. It's certainly not a standard that must be met, but personally, motherhood made me a better preacher and pastor. What an unexpected, holy surprise. When the time came for me to step up into my current role of lead pastor, I was startled, but I was also able to recognize that I had been ready for quite some time.

I would have never believed it if someone told me I would eventually start a church. I certainly would not have believed that six years into it I could be leading this beautiful, energetic, and open congregation. Surely, calling is what brought me here. But the calling has been a culmination of countless stories, both mine and those I've inherited from others, past and present. For example, the stories of my congregation teach me, give me wisdom, and show me how to be a pastor every day. Their stories continue to mold me and sustain me as I lead and look ahead.

My stories, along with those I've inherited, are responsible for shaping so much of what I bring to ministry. This includes a regard for church tradition and a love for the church calendar. It also explains my gravitation toward contemplative spiritual practice and my commitment to interfaith work and community. The stories of my life and the stories I have inherited also led me to the Baptist tradition. From within this tradition I have found deep meaning in local church autonomy and soul freedom, and I have discovered a great passion for religious liberty that continues to shape my calling. I have also found a home, a tribe, and a place to fully live out my call to ministry and the various callings of my life. In short, stories have made me who I am, and they continue to shape me, both as a person and a pastor.

People ask me about "call" often. What does it mean to be called to something? We are all called to things, whether those callings exist within or outside ministerial work. I believe our callings are ever evolving, and I also believe that our lives are made up of multiple callings, both big and small. It is our job to pay attention to the movement of the Spirit so that we can discern the work of God we are called to in this broken world.

What this tells me is that our most important call is to listen. Listen to the movement of our lives; look for God in our present moments. God exists in the here and now, and God can be known through the stories of our daily lives. Listening will help us know what we need to do next, and it will also remind us that *being* (meaning *belonging* to Christ) is more important than *doing*. Listening should precede doing, and when we are really listening, the doing will always be inevitable.

Listening as a spiritual practice is the best way I have understood calling throughout my own life. In seminary, people asked me often what I was called to after graduation. They wanted to know my plan, and my peers often seemed to have an answer ready when asked the same question. There's nothing wrong with having specific hopes and plans, but it isn't how I operate or how I have perceived God to work in my life.

I don't always feel sure about what call means, even in my own life. But I do know that right now I am called to the small but mighty community of believers at Peace of Christ Church. This is where I belong in this season, and I don't need the right words to explain it. Instead, my heart, soul, and gut tell me so every day. The Spirit of God dwelling within me tells me so. I am called to this work of creating safe, authentic, creative, questioning, faith-filled, worshipful space for all. This is the work I am compelled to do. Alongside our staff, leadership team and congregation, I am living out my call the best way I know how.

What does it mean to "live out" a calling? For me, it means putting one foot in front of the other. It means asking God for the continued provision of "daily bread." It means trying my best to listen well and then to do what is necessary, out of each present moment. The collision between sacred and ordinary, best revealed through the stories of our lives, has been such a gift to me throughout my journey. It is a powerful reminder that we all have a calling. We are all ordinary people called to the holy things of God. What we do with our lives matters, and often the small moments end up being the most significant ones. May the beautiful life of Jesus continue to show us the way each day, and may we be compelled to listen and then follow. Amen.

Aurelia Davila Pratt is the lead pastor at Peace of Christ Church in Round Rock, Texas. She serves on the advisory team for the "Nevertheless, She Preached" Conference and on the Baylor School of Social Work Board of Advocates, and was a 2017 Fellow of the Baptist Joint Committee for Religious Liberty. She is married to Lyle, and they have a young daughter, Cosette.

A Call as Real
as the Sunshine

Drew Prince

My father was a Southern Baptist minister who was fortunate enough to stay at the same church for 32 years. That was a gift to my family, since most preachers' kids get moved around like military families. But early on, I never dreamed that someday I would also be called to serve as a pastor.

Many children who grow up with ministers as parents have horror stories about how their parents were treated. My experience was just the opposite. My church was my home away from home and my extended family.

After college I spent seven years teaching high school and loved every minute of it. However, when I got married, I found that I could not fund a retirement account on a teacher's salary. When I was single, I wasn't concerned about next week, much less retirement. Once I became married, I decided I had to plan for the future.

For years I wondered if I could be successful in pharmaceutical sales, so I pursued that option. Within six months I got the opportunity. During those years I built up a retirement account so that one day I would be able to retire with dignity. What I did not realize at the time was that all of those years in teaching and sales were preparing me for ministry.

In February 2002 my wife, Kim, and I finally moved into the house that she wanted to stay in forever. Both of us were in pharmaceutical sales and making more money than we ever dreamed was possible. And both of us were completely unfulfilled doing it.

Public speaking always came very naturally to me. People began to ask me to do things such as give eulogies at funerals. Kim and I had started a Sunday School class at church that seemed to take on a life of its own. And in retrospect, I can see that all of this was building toward what happened next.

In my mind I wanted to return to my first love: teaching. But in my heart I knew that God was inviting me to pursue full-time ministry. There were no angels bouncing off the ceiling, but it was as real as the sunshine.

The time came when I explained to Kim what was happening. That conversation included both of us quitting our jobs and moving to Atlanta. Kim said that she would follow me anywhere. We gave up the company cars and the great jobs so that I could attend McAfee School of Theology and follow my calling.

Kim had one concern. We had been trying to have children unsuccessfully for four years. If and when we did, she wanted to be able to be a stay-at-home mom. I could only tell her that we would have to move forward on faith.

Kim got a new job in Atlanta, and we soon became pregnant with our first little girl. Kim went on maternity leave without any intention of going back. The week that her benefits ran out, I became the pastor of a little church in Atlanta. Then we added another little girl to our family. I know of no family that has been blessed more than we have.

Following our time in Atlanta, I spent the next four and a half years as the pastor of a church outside Louisville, Ky. This church had a history of ending its relationships with its pastors negatively. When the time came, I was the first pastor to leave that church on good terms in 23 years. And as God does, it was all in preparation for where I would be led next.

I am now the pastor of the church I grew up in and where my father served. He passed away long before I started this journey, but his influence is still strong in the spirit of our church.

Now my girls are experiencing what I did growing up. Our church is their home away from home and their extended family. I spent my childhood waiting for my parents to stop talking to the last people to exit the church each Sunday. Now I wait on my girls. They never want to leave!

Our church saw its share of pain before we came here several years ago. It had lost the pastor who followed my father, and in the aftermath also lost the associate pastor and secretaries. But the church somehow trusted in God that its best days had not passed.

As odd as it sounds, that conflict shaped my pastoral perspective and affirmed my sense of calling. While most people would run from such an experience, it revealed to me how my dad had navigated those kinds of waters all those years ago. It not only prepared me to lead our church in Kentucky through a few challenging circumstances, but it also influenced my eventual call to return home to serve as the pastor of West Hills Baptist Church, the church my dad had once served.

And now, thanks to the lessons I learned in those tough times and the faithfulness of the folks at West Hills, my children are experiencing at our church what I did growing up: a healthy church family that is a natural part of their spiritual lives. I can only hope their future holds the kind of fulfillment I have been so blessed to live.

Years before my children were born, I experienced all the good and all the bad a life in ministry can bring. But when it was all said and done, I can see God's hand in it every step along the way. It is incredible to look back. And now it is such a joy to look forward.

Our church is not perfect, but it is perfectly suited for my family. My experiences in teaching and in business add a different flavor to my ministry. My wife and my girls are happiest when they are with our church family. And what I see ahead is a gift—and it is as real as the sunshine!

Drew Prince is the senior pastor of the West Hills Baptist Church in Knoxville, Tenn. He and his wife Kim have two daughters, Grill and Elle. Their hearts belong to Jesus, but their blood runs Big Orange!

A Summons from God

David Sapp

The camp pastor had just asked us to consider whether God was calling us to a particular vocation. I was eight years old, and I felt a keen urge to respond. A boy sitting near me went forward and announced to the entire camp that God had called him to be a movie star. He assured us all that he wanted to surrender to God's will.

The other boys snickered, and I tried to disappear. The snickering ended any chance of going public with my feelings. I would just keep my urge to myself.

When I got home, though, the thoughts of a future in ministry did not go away. They rumbled around in my mind and occupied many of my prayers. Finally, one night I got out of bed, knelt, and promised God I would be a pastor.

I was afraid that no one would take me seriously. After all, I was only eight years old. I felt safe telling my parents and a few friends, but my decision did not go beyond that for several years. When adults would ask me what I wanted to be when I grew up, I would tell them honestly that I wanted to be a pastor. They invariably advised me to give it time since I might be mistaken. But I always felt that I was not mistaken. I could not imagine changing my mind.

These dubious attitudes persisted even into my seminary years, so much so that I did ask God from time to time whether I had misunderstood. Since I never heard him say that I had misunderstood, I kept to the path, although I, of course, asked questions. I somehow knew that a call from God, especially one perceived at such an early stage, is too serious a matter to pursue untested. But all the while, I found myself drawn to the words God spoke to Jeremiah, "Do not say, 'I am a boy,' for you shall go to all to whom I send you, and you shall speak whatever I command you" (Jer. 1:7-8). I was drawn also to the verse in which young Timothy was told, "Let no one despise your youth" (1 Tim. 4:12).

I have come to appreciate those who viewed my early call with skepticism. Anyone who claims to have heard the voice of God *should* be questioned, perhaps especially an eight-year-old. Too many people are already running around claiming they have a word from God when all they have is a word that comes from their own insecurity, anger, or fear. The Bible calls these people false prophets and seriously admonishes us to beware of them.

The experience I had when I was eight years old was a defining moment in my life. I heard a musician say recently that once he discovered music, he knew what he was put here to do. That is how I have felt about being a pastor. Once I discovered my calling, I knew what I was put here to do. Many people, of course, struggle with their call, or resist it. My own son has such a story, as you can read elsewhere in this book. Such struggles are very real and are to be deeply respected. But for some reason I do not understand, my call was never a struggle, only a thing to be embraced.

In time, people began to offer repeated confirmations of my call. I am not speaking of *affirmations*. My encouragers did not offer compliments so much as they offered observations that they had seen God working in me and that they too felt God was calling me.

The first such confirmation came from my grandfather. A Middle Georgia farmer with just seven years of formal education, Papa was profoundly wise. He and my grandmother did not have running water, and every evening he would make a trek to the spring and "tote" (as he said) two buckets of water back up the hill. The spring was at the bottom of a deep gully across the road from their house, so the walk back carrying two heavy buckets of water was a bit of a challenge in the Georgia heat.

Getting to accompany Papa on those trips to the spring was a treat for each of us grandchildren. On those walks we had him to ourselves. He would identify the birds whose songs we heard, he would teach us the names of the trees, or he would tell us a story. But best of all, on the way back up the hill, Papa would stop and sit on an old log to rest, and we would just talk.

On one such occasion, when I was the only grandchild along, we stopped at the "rest log" and had one of the most memorable conversations of my childhood. He told me that as a young boy he had an experience with sin that had wounded him for the rest of his life. He never told me what the experience was, but even a child could sense that it was an important event in his life. As a result of that encounter, he told me, he had prayed for God to use one of his children, as he said, "to fight sin."

"I believe," he went on, "that your call to ministry is God's answer to my prayer." Those were huge words spoken to me at an early age. They are some of the most important words anyone ever said to me.

My call took me down paths I could have scarcely imagined as a child. In seminary I served on the staff of one of the first racially integrated Baptist churches. I attained a PhD in Christian Ethics. I worked to mobilize Baptists against hunger as a staff member at our denomination's social ethics agency. During more than 30 years as a pastor I did my best to confront evil, proclaim justice, and help members of my congregation to get free from the dark forces in their lives. I came to think my grandfather's words about fighting sin were rustic and backwoods, but every now and then I would pause to think about what I was doing. I could never escape the notion that, in some small way, I was fighting sin.

These confirmations did not end with my grandfather. As I matured, I found internal confirmation. I discovered that I cared about people, and that I actually enjoyed administration. I discovered that I loved preaching and was strangely free of the fear of public speaking. I discovered that I wanted to lead, and that most of the time I had a vision for the churches I served. My gifts and inclinations, it turned out, fit what I felt called to do, and they confirmed for me that my perception as an eight-year-old of what God intended for me was right on target.

The churches of which I was a part also confirmed my call. Ardsley Park Baptist Church in Savannah, Ga., gave me my first opportunities to preach as a youth and blessed my excited, if stumbling, efforts. While I was just a college sophomore the Adgateville Baptist Church near Monticello, Ga., called me as pastor, and those patient people accepted a young preacher's first efforts at being a pastor.

Every church I served afterward added a similar blessing. Churches tend to shape ministers as much as ministers shape churches. Each church called me, encouraged me, believed in me, forgave me, followed me, led me, broke me, healed me, prayed for me, and embraced me. In so doing, those churches made me more fit for ministry. They gave me confidence for the journey, and they enlarged my vision of the destination. On many days they put me on their shoulders and carried me. Every time they did this, they confirmed me as a minister and contributed to a culture of calling within the church.

I am 70 now and have lived with this calling since I was just eight. Life has taught me a lot about ministry, but a couple of things stand out. For one, I have learned that calling is not an honor, but a mission. God says, "Here is a world of need." He puts his hand on our shoulder, gives us a nudge—sometimes gentle and sometimes not—and says, "Go." Calling is not the conferral of a status; it is a summons to change the world.

I have learned another thing about calling. This sense of being summoned by the Divine One, of being addressed by the voice of God, is, in itself, the power for the mission. The call is not one thing and the power to fulfill it another. The call *is* the power. When the "dark night of the soul" has fallen upon me, when the mission has seemed impossible, when the forces of darkness have massed in my path, God's call has given me power. I have learned that I am not simply a human; I am a human called by God. I stand by the power of God. I live by the power of God. I minister by the power of God. I fight sin by the power of God. After all, Jesus promised, "You will receive power when the Holy Spirit has come upon you; and you will be my witnesses" (Acts 1:8a).

In the last few years before I retired, this power became evident to me to a degree I had never before experienced. Sin put on a face, strode across my path, looked me in the eye, and threatened the life of my church and the security of my pastorate. I became convinced all over again that the devil is real, that evil has a life of its own, and that its power is greater than mine. Like the psalmist, I sometimes felt that evil people were stalking me (Psalms 54, 55, 56). I had met the devil, up close and personal, and I found him to be the most fearsome and frightening terror of all.

Some of my friends counseled me to resign from my church. Then a woman stopped after church one Sunday and said, "You do know that God has sent you here for such an hour as this?" In my soul a voice said that she was right. Frankly, at the time I wished God had sent someone else, but he had not. I repeated to myself the words spoken to Joshua after the death of Moses: "As I was with Moses, so I will be with you; I will not fail you or forsake you" (Josh. 1:5). And once again I took comfort from the memory of a long-ago visit with an old man trudging back to his daily life from a spring. It was as though he was still speaking and said, "You were called to fight sin, not run from it."

Others may wonder whether God really speaks to people, really calls people. It sounds bizarre, I know. But for me, my call has been the source of my purpose in life and the strength to pursue it. It has been vision in darkness, hope in discouragement, and power in weakness. It has been joy in the morning, at noontime, and in the evening. It has been food for my soul. It has been not just any calling, but the high calling of God in Christ Jesus. This is the story of my call. Thanks be to God.

David Sapp is a retired pastor and ethicist who lives in Atlanta, Ga. He began his career at the former Christian Life Commission of the Southern Baptist Convention, and retired in 2012 as the senior pastor of Second-Ponce de Leon Baptist Church in Atlanta. He and his wife Linda are the enthusiastic grandparents of four young grandsons.

Like a Fish Out of Water

Matt Sapp

I first expressed a feeling that I'd been called to ministry about the time I graduated from high school in 1997. My family lived in Richmond, Va., at the time, and I wrote a letter to my dad, a pastor himself, telling him that I thought God was leading me in that direction. A letter seemed easier; I wasn't sure I was up for a face-to-face conversation.

That first sense of calling was shaped by experiences in Sunday morning worship as a teenager, youth group devotionals, and summer discipleship camps as I moved through high school. And, even though the two experiences are separated by hundreds of miles and nearly a decade in time, my experience of calling continues to be intimately connected in my mind to my experience of salvation.

My sense of calling has never been easy for me to articulate. My experience of God and calling contains enough mysticism that words often seem to fall short. But as I think about that first sense of calling, I remember feeling a very strong desire—as many young people do—to do something that would make a difference in the world. And as that feeling grew in me, I developed a sense that God was shaping my abilities and blessing me with experiences that left me well suited for a future in ministry.

While some things about my calling are difficult to put into words, I can say one thing clearly: From the very beginning, I wasn't comfortable with it. I didn't want to be a pastor. I didn't want to work in a church. In fact, having grown up in a pastor's family, it was probably the last thing I wanted to do.

I'm still not comfortable with it all the time.

So, after first articulating a call to ministry at the age of 18, I spent the next decade doing everything possible *not* to follow God's call on my life.

My story of calling is a story like Jonah's. God called, I heard, and I fled in the opposite direction. It's not an overstatement to say that I ran as far away from God in as many ways as I could when I heard God's voice.

When God called Jonah to the city of Nineveh, Jonah boarded a ship to Tarshish as quickly as he could, knowing that Tarshish was as far as one could possibly go in the opposite direction. My story couldn't be more like that if I wanted it to be.

As Jonah fled to Tarshish, it wasn't long before he faced great storms that would test his faith and cast doubt on the direction he had chosen. My experience was the same. After first articulating a call to ministry, I spent 10 directionless years doing all kinds of things that kept me from moving any closer to the life God intended for me. During that time, I started and stopped attending school four different times at three different colleges. Between those stints in school I worked and wandered, moving increasingly farther from the path to which God had called me.

The great storms Jonah faced on board the ship, though, were not the worst of his experience. Before long, Jonah found himself alone and drowning in a storm-tossed sea, rescued only by God's providence in the form of a great fish that swallowed him whole and spit him out on dry ground.

The prayer of Jonah as God rescued him, recorded in Jonah 2:2-9, became my prayer, too, as I struggled to find my way back to God's calling:

In my distress I called to the LORD, and he answered me. From deep in the realm of the dead I called for help, and you listened to my cry. You hurled me into the depths, into the very heart of the seas, and the currents swirled about me; all your waves and breakers swept over me. I said, "I have been banished from your sight; yet I will look again toward your holy temple." The engulfing waters threatened me, the deep surrounded me; seaweed was wrapped around my head. To the roots of the mountains I sank down; the earth beneath barred me in forever. But you, LORD my God, brought my life up from the pit. When my life was ebbing away, I remembered you, LORD, and my prayer rose to you, to your holy temple. Those who cling to worthless idols turn away from God's love for them. But I, with shouts of grateful praise, will sacrifice to you. What I have vowed I will make good. I will say, "Salvation comes from the LORD."

I know what it means to say, "the deep surrounded me" (v. 6). I know what Jonah meant when he confessed, "my life was ebbing away" (v. 7). Like Jonah, I prayed to God, and God rescued me. Through family and friends, God rescued me. My calling as a pastor is the calling of one who can honestly say, "God brought my life up from the pit. If God can rescue me, God can rescue you, too."

At the end of a 10-year odyssey, I graduated from Mercer University with a degree in Christianity and political science, but I still wasn't sure about pursuing a life in local church ministry. Instead, I moved to Washington, D.C., intending to use my political science background to chase a career in foreign service or public policy.

While I was in Washington, I was invited to join a men's Bible study group by a friend from Mercer who had also moved to Washington. And it was in this seemingly random Bible study with a seemingly random assortment of six or seven young men from all over the country that I felt the final tug on my life to become a local church minister.

After a brief stay in Washington, I answered God's call to ministry by enrolling at Mercer University's McAfee School of Theology in Atlanta.

I've never felt quite as much like a fish out of water as I did those first few weeks at seminary. My story didn't match the stories of the others there. I'd taken a significantly different path and brought with me a significantly different set of life experiences. I wasn't as sure of my calling as others in my classes.

Despite growing up in church, I wasn't as knowledgeable about the Bible as others were. I wasn't as experienced in ministry or church leadership. I'd never chaperoned a youth retreat or been a counselor at summer camp. I hadn't spent my college years interning at a local church. I couldn't tell you where the Baptist Student Union was on campus if my life depended on it. I hadn't even been to Sunday School in more than a decade.

Everything about the people by whom I was now surrounded was foreign to me. But over time I came to feel more comfortable around people who were more comfortable with their ministry identities than I was. I read theology and loved it. I thought deeply about the words of Jesus in the Gospels and was changed by them. I discovered a richness to the stories of the Old Testament that continues to amaze me.

I needed every second of my three years in seminary to grow comfortable with my calling. Even more importantly, I needed those three years to move beyond the spiritual disorientation associated with my decade of rebellion.

While I was studying in seminary, still with no discernable experience or qualification for ministry, Wieuca Road Baptist Church in Atlanta was brave enough to let me be their part-time youth minister, and I was naïve enough to accept. I remember sitting at my desk that first day on the job wondering what on earth I'd gotten myself into, with no idea what I was supposed to do.

Wieuca Road gave me my first opportunities to test whether my giftedness fit my calling. I figured out how to make a hospital visit and lead a committee meeting. I got my first opportunities to lead in worship and plan a ministry calendar. I learned to work with volunteer Sunday School teachers and youth camp chaperones. I prepared and delivered my first sermons. And when I graduated from seminary, Wieuca Road gave me my first full-time church job and ordained me into the ministry. Two years later I moved on to serve my first church as lead pastor. I am now in my second pastorate.

Even today, though, I continue to ask: "What is God's purpose for me? How does God intend to use me? Am I where God wants me to be, doing what God wants me to do? And, if not, where should I be, what should I be doing, and how do I get there?"

I've come to understand calling as a process of listening for direction, trusting intuition, and approaching the work God puts in front of me with energy, excellence, and faith. As I grow into my calling, I realize more each day that God's claim on my life is total—that I belong to God intimately and completely—and that as part of my calling I belong not only to God, but also to the work and the communities for which God has shaped me.

Most days in ministry I find myself painfully aware that I am a work in progress, so I pray almost every day that God will continue to create in me, and that God will continue to create through me, as the world for which Christ died continues to look more like God's kingdom.

Matt Sapp is the pastor of Central Baptist Church in Newnan, Ga., having previously served churches in Canton and Atlanta. He and his wife, Julie, stay busy parenting their two young sons.

"Can Boys Be Preachers?"

Sarah Jackson Shelton

She came out from behind her parents to hand me her bulletin. She had drawn a portrait. It was clearly of me: glasses, short hair, a robe, and an open mouth! Her mother pulled me aside to say that her eight-year-old asked a very important question during worship: "Can boys be preachers or just girls?" My heart soared.

You see, being a "preacher girl" in the 1980s was not such a positive thing in Baptist circles. It is hardly popular now! But calling can spur us on to do some unlikely and courageous things.

I was a rising senior, and the church youth choir in which I sang was on tour somewhere in Florida. I slipped out of my hotel room to pray on the steps. "Take this unsettled feeling away from me, God. I will do anything to get rid of it. I will even be your minister." With that last admission, the unrest left. A sense of calming assurance filled me with such a recognizable presence that I have repeatedly felt at pivotal moments in my journey: at the Sea of Galilee, the labyrinth at Sacred Heart monastery, the National Cathedral, and the American Church in Paris. That night in Florida was my first step of walking the journey with God. I set my course.

The only position I had ever seen a female take on a church staff was director of kindergarten. So, I majored in early childhood education at the University of Alabama and arrived at the Southern Baptist Theological Seminary for a Master of Religious Education. My thoughts about calling and my role in it changed the very first semester, however.

I set an appointment with Dr. Findley Edge and told him I was feeling led in a different direction. When he questioned me about it, I was hesitant but confided, "I have never seen it done before." He immediately positioned himself so that we were knee to knee. He held both of my hands and looked me in the eye. "Wouldn't you rather be a part of something new than be a part of what has always been?" he asked. Everything within me said yes. In addition to affirmation from other professors, I knew I was on the right track when I was selected the winner of the Francisco Preaching Award.

Two masters' degrees later, I came to Birmingham to be a youth minister. I arrived in June of 1981, just a few short weeks before the Southern Baptist Convention passed resolutions crediting women for all the sin in the world and decrying that no woman may serve as a senior pastor. The church in which I served, however, ordained and licensed me. Another female was called to be a staff minister, and she was licensed and ordained too.

The climate of the SBC continued down a negative path, and when a man in the church was appointed as a trustee to the International Mission Board, our local congregation began to struggle. The Cooperative Baptist Fellowship was formed, and I was asked to serve on the first coordinating council. When my name was published in *The Alabama Baptist* as a member of the council, a church member called to say that if I did not resign my involvement with CBF, then from the floor of a business meeting he would ask for my resignation as youth minister. My response? "I guess you will have to ask for my resignation." As you can well imagine, there was a flurry of activity to smooth things over. Guest speakers came. Town hall meetings were held. But in the end, and after 11 years of service, I was not forgiven for bringing "the controversy" into this local church. I packed my office in the dark of night.

I have been asked many times since, "Why didn't you align with a different denomination? Why didn't you just give in?" And my answer is, "Calling. I am called to be a Christian. I am called to be a Baptist (in the best sense of that word). I am called to be a preaching pastor." If there has been one consistent element of my story, it is calling; calling that ebbs and flows; calling that needles and pries; calling that is vibrantly alive, changing, and growing.

It is calling that ultimately moved me out of the church. Realizing that I had worked in churches for almost 20 years and still did not have a pulpit, I finally told God, "I have done everything I know to do. You called me to preach, and if you are true to that calling, then you will get off your throne and make it happen." I was home for nine months, a gestation period, when Baptist Church of the Covenant (BCOC) contacted me.

I knew this church. I was 13, living in Birmingham with my father, a Baptist minister, and my mother, a stalwart of the Woman's Missionary Union, when BCOC formed. The word on the street was that this new church start was created by a bunch of rebels who dared to open their doors to African Americans. Their beginning took place in 1970, and, ever since, their doors have been open to anyone who desires to worship Jesus Christ as Lord.

Initially, BCOC just needed an intentional interim, but it provided me an opportunity to preach every Sunday for an entire year. This was followed by another nine-month period wherein BCOC did a national search for a new pastor. After the Calling Committee asked the congregation to change their policy that an interim could not be called as a new pastor, the committee came back to me in August of 2002 asking me to be the pastor. I agreed.

Local and international media picked up the story. A couple from the congregation was at the International Mission Board asking for an appointment as volunteer missionaries to Africa. They were denied, because their home church (BCOC) had just called a female as senior pastor. Rocks came through the windows of the church building. The Birmingham Baptist Association summoned me before the Membership Committee, and three times the leadership met with me behind closed doors. I kept reminding them that they knew who I was, for I was a product of their making, having been raised in this same association and having served churches of this association for 21 years. It did not matter because I was a female, a fact over which I had no control or choice! After the associational missionary told the congregation of BCOC that he would never hire an ordained woman or a person who was LGBTQ, BCOC voted to disassociate completely from the Southern Baptist Convention, the Alabama State Convention, and the Birmingham Baptist Association.

This sort of limelight "controversy" was not new to BCOC. Members of that congregation are veterans of what is required to step out in faith to bring change that speaks to social justice. Their courage to welcome "all" brought my understanding of how diversity is possible in a family of faith. Each time new members are presented here, we read a litany of corporate and personal commitments to reaffirm together that we will care for one another and that our doors will be open to all. The full meaning of "all" is experienced weekly.

BCOC is a community where LGBTQ members use their gifts in service to God and to one another. It is where those who are illiterate sit in worship with those who have earned PhDs. It is where the elderly, alone or forgotten by their families, are cared for through support teams. It is where foster children are treasured and nurtured. It is where the homeless eat Wednesday night supper while being seated next to accomplished professionals. This congregation's sense of calling to welcome all and to tenaciously be a beacon of hope on the south side of Birmingham continues to challenge my calling to grow in gracious hospitality. I could not have fulfilled my calling without the BCOC congregation who allows me a pulpit of complete freedom.

I could not have fulfilled my calling without the support of my family either. While he does not have a designated parking space, my husband, Lloyd, takes great pride in being the "first lady." The congregation affectionately calls him "Big Mama." His support is unswerving, his loyalty remains constant even when I am a bundle of insecurity, and his sense of humor sees us through many challenges. Our children, David and Dannelly, have done their part too. Now adults, Dannelly has returned to Birmingham and is serving on three church committees! And David? He lives in New York City with his partner. With the loving acceptance and influence of BCOC, when he "came out" we were able to embrace him totally and completely as our son.

I am learning every day that calling is mutual. God calls us and, in our relationship with God, that call continues to grow and develop. A church calls us to serve and, in relationship with church family, that call joins together the most unlikely of lives to provide vision for the Kingdom. Calling is what brings inspiration for sermons. Calling is what opens our hearts to hear the stories of the brokenhearted. Calling keeps us going when we have stood in the graveyard one time too many. Calling keeps us putting one foot in front of the other when we walk the hospital hallways of surgery and chronic illness. Calling keeps hope alive when everyone else says, "You can't do that." If I am to be remembered for anything, I hope and pray that my life is a testimony to faithfulness—faithfulness to a call that would not let me go.

Sarah Jackson Shelton is married to Lloyd Shelton. They have two sons, David and Dannelly. Now retired, she served as the senior pastor of Baptist Church of the Covenant in Birmingham, Ala., from 2002 to 2019.

A Calling Adventure

William D. Shiell

According to the Auburn Institute, God calls persons to serve the church through churches. In other words, pastors and congregations call ministers to ministry. For me, calling is an ongoing adventure. I never expected to be called, and God has always led me in surprisingly unexpected ways—never where or how I planned. The one constant has been the voice of the church.

Evangelicals describe salvation as an event when Jesus "comes into your heart." As a child, I prayed a similar formulaic prayer as many times as possible; but the church saved my life. As Jesus did for the disciples on the Emmaus Road, Christians "caught me from behind" and shared a word from Christ. They opened my eyes to see the risen Christ in the breaking of the bread and the fellowship around the table. They redirected my path to follow the adventure of God's call.

My dad died in 1983 when I was a 10-year-old child. My pastor, Brian Harbour, visited my home, comforted me in grief, and conducted my dad's funeral. A year later I professed faith at a middle school camp in Chula Vista, Ala. A few weeks later Dr. Harbour baptized me at First Baptist Church in Pensacola, Fla., during a Sunday evening service. The church had protected me through the storms of grief. Now the church accompanied me into the adventure of faith.

In 1987 I attended Centrifuge Camp at North Greenville College (now Greenville University) in South Carolina, a high school camp conducted by the Southern Baptist Sunday School Board. A young college student named Kyle Matthews led worship. As a ninth grader, I sang in his choir and listened like Samuel for God's voice. After walking to the front during a worship service invitation, my counselor handed me a pre-printed card, indicating the ways God "called" people into ministry: pastor, music minister, missionary, and so forth. Even then I knew my calling didn't fit into a box. I checked a few categories on the form and marked another milestone on the calling journey.

My church gave me the opportunity to practice this calling. Mrs. K.K. Knight invited me to lead the "devotional" for her Sunday School department. (Apparently, the small group classes needed a sermon before the lesson.) Music Minister Bob Morrison gave me a job in the music ministry stamping choir octavos and building cases for sound systems.

Simultaneously, I attended a fundamentalist Christian school. Despite my later disagreements with their theology, this place became part of the soil that nurtured my faith. I memorized (a lot of) King James Version scriptures and preached in chapel.

My hard-working mother always encouraged me but never offered advice. When asked, she told me to pray about my decisions and to choose a path that would leave doors open for the future. I followed her wisdom on my first big move to college.

Samford University and the Alabama Baptist Convention invited me on the next adventure. Their religion major scholarships made college affordable. Gene Black and the Samford A Cappella Choir gave me the opportunity three college summers out of four to conduct mission work in Germany after the Berlin Wall fell. My senior year I served on a music team encouraging new church plants throughout former East Germany.

While at Samford I worked with the music and college ministries at Dawson Memorial Baptist Church where Gary Fenton was the pastor. I interned under a large church staff. I also met my future wife Kelly through the college ministry; she immediately shared and embraced the calling of pastoral ministry.

Samford faculty shaped my calling to the church and the classroom. John Killinger taught preaching for a few years at Samford. After my first sermon he told me that I needed to grow a little older before I preached that one again. Dennis Sansom took me and 15 other students to study at the Baptist seminary in Rüschlikon, Switzerland. We arrived the week that the Southern Baptist Foreign Mission Board cut its funding because Rüschlikon was considered too "liberal." On that trip the scales of my childhood faith began to fall off. I began to follow Jesus with a new vision of young adult faith. I saw clearly the darkness of right-wing fundamentalism. I met theologian Jürgen Moltmann, visited the Dachau concentration camp, and learned a way of following Christ that has pursued me ever since.

Since most of my pastors studied in Texas, I assumed I would go to Southwestern Baptist Theological Seminary in Fort Worth. But after the seminary's trustees terminated Russell Dilday's presidency, Samford's university minister Paul Basden told me about a new seminary starting at Baylor University: George W. Truett Theological Seminary. With the support of the Piper Foundation, Cooperative Baptist Fellowship, the Baptist General Convention of Texas, and Eastern Star, I graduated from seminary debt free. Ironically, I took preaching from Russell Dilday and "Life and Work of the Pastor" from Brian Harbour as a student at Truett.

While in Waco, Texas, I served on the staff of First Baptist Church of Lorena for three years and Meadowbrook Baptist Church of Waco for a semester. I learned from Pastor Mike Patterson the importance of resourcefulness and from my choirs the significance of organization and building relationships with people first. Brother Mike allowed me to preach monthly on Sunday evenings.

My last semester at Truett, I took a PhD-level seminar in Acts from my eventual advisor in the doctoral program, Mikeal Parsons. That fall I began PhD studies as a New Testament student in the religion department of Baylor University. I had a clear call to teach and preach, and I was learning to shelve my plans.

I assumed (again wrongly) that right after seminary, churches would be lined up to ask me to be their pastor. But after 25 rejections from just about every church in a 100-mile radius of

Waco, I left Lorena and joined the staff of Meadowbrook Baptist Church. There Eric Holleyman taught me how to weave messages through music and sermons.

First Baptist Church of McGregor, Texas, called me to serve as pastor in January 1999. There I learned to preach from memory and to love people. My wife made strawberry bread for every family in the church, and I personally delivered a loaf to each home. We also held our first open house, a tradition we continued for 17 years. I completed coursework at Baylor and prepared to take preliminary exams. Then a surprise came along the way.

Jesse Fletcher, at the time chancellor of Hardin-Simmons University and interim pastor of Southland Baptist Church in San Angelo, recommended me as Southland's pastor. The "call" process moved quickly. Southland taught me the value of women serving equally as deacons and pastoral staff with men. There I also learned the significance of lay leadership and faced my first routine management and systems challenges that are part of every church. I began to see my blind spots and the challenge of living with high expectations.

What I began in San Angelo I carried forward to three other churches. I discovered that God seemed to call me to churches that were in debt from building campaigns, facing worship challenges, and struggling with defining their identity as moderate Baptists.

My first son Parker was born in San Angelo. I published my dissertation with E.J. Brill in the Biblical Interpretation series, thanks to Mike Parsons and his wife Heidi Hornik, who also served on my dissertation committee. Howard Payne University asked me to be an instructor in its adult learning program. (Little did I know that these adult learners would preview what was to come later in my life.)

Jesse Fletcher then recommended me to his former church, First Baptist Church of Knoxville, Tenn. I served there nine years and had my first taste of what life would be like as both pastor and professor. I taught undergraduate-level material to a church that, as former pastor Doug Watterson remarked, had a "ministry of the mind." I also learned the importance of stewardship and fundraising, a skill that would serve me well later.

In 2010 David Crutchley invited me to serve as adjunct professor of religion at Carson-Newman University in Jefferson City, just outside Knoxville, and to teach New Testament to undergrads. The experience of writing and teaching the lectures helped me articulate my theology and prepare me for a future calling. I published two books and learned to balance pastoring a region through live television ministry.

My second son Drake was born in Knoxville, and we still consider this place "home" for our family. I performed the Gospel of Mark from memory and discovered a group of "performance critics" who study how an oral reading of the Bible affected interpretation. Our church ordained three women to gospel ministry. Two of them have since been called to be a senior pastor.

My half-brother, his wife, and my two nephews also entered my life unexpectedly. Although space does not permit to tell the full story, this unexpected blessing became yet another example that my calling and ministry would be full of surprises beyond my planning.

First Baptist Church in Tallahassee, Fla., called in 2012. That church taught me how to minister in a different Florida than the one where I was born. I learned to preach two different styles on the same Sunday—one for a mature audience who had heard many sermons in their lives, the other for a learning audience eager to soak up the truths of faith. I also bumped into the deep unhealed wounds of racial division in the South that would become a part of a future ministry. A capital city torn apart by gun violence, partisanship, and racial friction served as a training ground.

When biblical scholar Scot McKnight came to Tallahassee to lead a conference on the gospel, I had no idea what lay ahead for me. The president of Northern Seminary in Chicago was about to announce his retirement, and Scot asked me to consider going to Northern. After my initial "no," Northern kept calling; and I realized this was God's way of fulfilling my dormant decision from ninth grade—one that didn't fit a box on a card at a Baptist camp. This was the calling to the classroom and the congregation—just as a seminary president.

Northern is an institution called to love the city and to train pastoral leaders in the midst of gun violence, racial injustice, campus secularism, rural opiate crises, and church decline. The students are like the adult learner-pastors I first taught at Howard Payne. Most of our leadership challenges are the same ones I faced at McGregor and Knoxville—without the safety net of weekly offerings. I teach preaching and New Testament and raise money so that other students may have the same experience of seminary I had—free from debt and empowered to serve the church and engage the world.

My family has now shifted roles from "pastor's family" to a normal, church-going family. On my journey, pastors, ministers, and laity have entered my life providentially as models for ministry. I watched them preach and struggle. They showed me that ministry is challenging yet extremely rewarding. They taught me to endure public critiques, remain calm, and persevere. They gave me courage. They taught me to preach from memory and offer pastoral care. They invited me into their lives and challenged me when I was too presumptuous. They showed me why church and faith don't fit neatly into a box. My past is a curriculum for present opportunities.

Brian Harbour advised me in seminary that when discerning God's call, I would never really know for sure whether to accept a call to somewhere new until I arrived there, looked back, and saw God at work closing doors behind me and opening doors in front of me. Faith is an adventure best lived discerning that calling. On the way, Jesus surprises me in life's journey and continues to open my eyes to his presence through his church.

William Shiell currently serves as the president of Northern Seminary in Chicago, Ill. He previously served as the senior pastor of churches in Texas, Tennessee, and Florida. A graduate of Samford University in Birmingham, Ala., he also holds MDiv and PhD degrees from Baylor University's Truett Theological Seminary. He and his wife, Kelly, have two sons.

"Phoebe After All . . ."

Chris Smith

I feel a strong connection to God's word spoken to Jeremiah, "Before I formed you in the womb I knew you, and before you were born I consecrated you; I have appointed you a prophet to the nations" (Jer. 1:5, NASB).

Before marriage, my mother almost became a nun. Upon leaving the convent, she prayed that the Lord would call one of her children. I believe I am that child.

My mom fondly recalls that before becoming pregnant with me, she had a dream that her fraternal grandmother told her she would have a girl and that the girl should be named "Phoebe." I remember as a little girl, sitting with my mom as she frequently recounted that story to me—a story I heard all of my life.

Although my mom forgot about the dream and instead named me "Christine," the dream had profound implications. According to Romans 16:1, Phoebe was a servant/leader in the church. It is my belief that the dream foreshadowed God's calling upon my life.

My parents instilled in each of their children the importance of living lives pleasing to Almighty God, getting a good education and becoming responsible, respectful, honest people. My parents' teaching helped me to develop a strong Christian faith that is an integral part of my vision for life and ministry. As I look back over those years, I realize that my mother was unable to fulfill her calling within her religion (Catholicism) but hoped that her call would be answered through her offspring.

Although I was raised Catholic, through a series of events I ended up attending church with a Baptist friend. At the age of 15 I joined the church and was baptized. Within a year I was working with the Christian education department, helping to design and display bulletin boards, writing and directing Easter and Christmas programs, singing in the choir, and working as an assistant teacher.

When I was 16, God spoke to my heart and called me to preach. Praise God that when I went to my pastor, he did not discourage me because I am a woman. I was initially uncomfortable with the idea, but my pastor assured me he would pray with and for me and that the Lord would lead me in the way I should go. About a year later I preached my initial sermon and was licensed in my home church.

After college I entered seminary and earned the Master of Divinity degree. Two aspects of my seminary training helped shape my ministry: (1) a research assistantship in the Bible Department and (2) an internship in the Black Women in Church and Society Program. In the BWCS program I worked with homeless women, helping them to obtain food and shelter. I also worked as a student counselor in an at-risk youth program in Atlanta, Ga.

As I grew in the ministry, I realized that God was calling me to become a pastor. It was not my first choice or desire, if I am honest. The "call," however, is not something one chooses—it chooses you! Like Jacob wrestled with the angel, I wrestled with God about the ministry. Truth be told, I simply wanted to go to school, get a decent job, get married, have children, and live happily ever after. God had another plan.

Originally, I wanted to pursue doctoral studies immediately after seminary. I was offered a slot in a Th.D. (Doctor of Theology) program at Boston University. I was thrilled! The same week, however, I was offered a position back home in the church where I initially accepted my call to the ministry. My heart sank. I felt God's strong direction to go back home and serve as an assistant pastor. It was one of the most difficult decisions I ever had to make—to release my dream and accept the pastoral call.

Interestingly, I did not experience the reality of the stained-glass ceiling or the ugliness of sexism in the church until years later. My initial assignment was filled with love, support, and opportunity. Even as I preached in various Baptist churches throughout the greater Cleveland/ Akron area, I was welcomed with open arms. I was considered by four local Baptist churches (two African-American and two Euro-American). Ultimately, I was called by a Euro-American congregation that had been without a pastor for three years.

The church had been in decline for a number of years. The membership was predominantly "gray" (65 and older), with a few younger adults and children. After much prayer and consideration, I accepted the call to the church and our journey together began. While I am convinced that we all desired to grow together and to have a multicultural ministry, the reality of melding cultures together is a difficult task—one that requires more than good intentions. Specific strategic planning is required.

Racism loomed large. As people from the surrounding areas began to join, mostly African Americans, the original members began to leave. Church leaders approached me with concerns that the church was "becoming too black." We invited guest speakers, engaged denominational consultants, held workshops, conducted listening sessions, prayed, did home visits, struggled, and cried. None of the efforts prevailed. The church that had gone from 40 members to more than 100 members in a year soon dwindled back down to 35 or 40 members. Finances caved. Ministry endeavors were severely cut back. Morale was crushed. I lost all benefits and my salary. Discouraged, new members began to leave. We almost died!

At the time I did not understand the dynamics that were at play beyond racism. I didn't know that women still only comprise approximately 11 percent of senior level pastoral positions across all Protestant denominations (per *Duke Today*, 2015). I didn't realize that even when a woman is called to a senior pastorate, her place of service will likely be a small, economically depressed, dysfunctional, and dying church. I didn't understand the complexities associated with being called as the pastor of a church from another culture. All of these factors greatly impacted my pastoral experience. However, good emerged from my intense and painful struggle.

As a result of my experience, I began to wonder about that of other female pastors. I began to conduct research on the experiences of my female clergy colleagues. I surveyed more than 100 female senior pastors regarding the pressures of ministry in the local church. I asked the pastors to respond to a series of statements regarding their common experiences. In response to the statement, "I find myself wearing many hats to handle the day-to-day operation of the church," an overwhelming 83 percent indicated that they strongly or moderately agreed. While "wearing many hats" means different things to different people, the image reflects that of a juggling act!

In general, women tend to be multitaskers. Because women tend to pastor smaller, struggling churches that are often financially unstable with minimal human and monetary resources, they end up sacrificing themselves to get things done. Many use their own money to fund activities, pay church bills, and support mission efforts. Frequently they have no associate staff or laypersons who are willing to help conduct necessary matters of church operation. Female pastors are likely to serve in the roles of preacher, pastoral caregiver, conductor of church meetings, church receptionist, developer and printer of bulletins, visitor of the sick—and the one tasked with raising the dead! This does not include the additional and important roles they may play outside of the church—daughter, wife, mother, sister, and friend—plus their involvement in other community activities and associations.

My own personal experience correlated strongly with the experiences of my sisters. I found myself struggling against depression, fatigue, and burnout. In spite of all of these things, the pastoral call burned ever strongly in my heart. I felt the call so prominently that I never considered giving up or leaving the ministry.

I attribute my survival to much prayer, support from family and friends, and my conviction that God was with me through it all. The belief that God was starting a new thing in the midst of the dearth kept me moving forward. At every turn I was provided a sprig of hope, new life, and a persistent vision of forthcoming change.

I must confess that "change" didn't look like what I thought it would. I was looking for, hoping for, praying for a surge in numerical growth, a rebirth of ministries now dead, and an overall "resurrection" testimony. Instead, the Lord provided us with a new paradigm for ministry.

We launched a stewardship program that encouraged "stewardship of life." We taught the importance of using our time, talent, and treasure to honor God and to do the work of God's Kingdom. We stressed the importance of tithing and putting God first in our lives.

Through strong stewardship, creative ministry efforts and grants, we were able to pay off the church's major debts. We also made the radical decision to sell our property and find a location to minister that was more conducive to our current structure. Our finances stabilized, my salary was reasonably restored, and the stress of financial duress has been lifted.

Although my congregation remains very small, it has grown by leaps and bounds in terms of ministry engagement, collaborative community efforts, social justice engagement, and leadership/discipleship development. Our work together extends far beyond our "four walls."

We have launched an annual initiative called "Healthy Temples: Supporting Healthy Minds, Bodies, and Spirits." Through this effort we have been blessed to cultivate a collaborative community effort with a local hospital, the county health board, a local grocery store, and other churches to address food deserts and food insecurities in our area.

My original curiosity evolved into a blog, *Shepastor*, and, ultimately, a book, *Beyond the Stained Glass Ceiling: Equipping and Encouraging Female Pastors*. Over the past decade I have been blessed to listen and learn from the experiences of my fellow clergy sisters from across ages, denominations, and cultures. Opportunities to conduct workshops, lectures, small groups, and conferences have emerged.

When I think back to my beginnings and my desire to simply go to school, get a "decent" job, get married, and have children, God granted all of that and also called me to serve as a pastor, leader, author, and blogger! Like a beautiful gift carefully packaged, God "packages us" and allows life to slowly unwrap the layers until the gifts inside emerge. My dream was exchanged for God's dream, and in that I have discovered the true desires of my heart. I am Phoebe after all!

Christine A. Smith is the pastor of Covenant Baptist Church in Euclid, Ohio, and the author of Beyond the Stained Glass Ceiling: Equipping and Encouraging Female Pastors *(Judson Press, 2013). Her weekly blog, "Shepastor" (http://Shepastor.blogspot.com), offers words of encouragement, wisdom, and insights for female clergy, Chris and her husband and three children live in Shaker Heights, Ohio.*

From Prodigal to Pastor

Joel Snider

I have often imagined an interview with an aged prodigal son and a reporter asking about his life in a *60 Minutes* format. Life has changed since he walked away from his father's house as a rebellious young man. The father who welcomed him home is now gone. His own hair is grayer than his father's was on the day the old man ran to greet him. He and his brother settled scores long ago and are now business partners.

Most of the questions are typical: "What went through your mind as you left home? How did you feel when you 'came to yourself'?"

Then comes the climax of the interview: "If you had it to do over again, would you take the inheritance and leave home?"

The once prodigal son thinks for a moment before answering. Would he choose riotous living and feeding pigs again? Never. But without that journey, would he have ever come to himself? Would he have ever come home to the grace that waited for him?

Tentatively he answers, "Knowing where I ended up, yes, I would. I'd do it again. But I wouldn't recommend it to others as a good way to find yourself."

I offer that fictionalized sequel to the parable of Jesus as a preface to the story of my call. I feel similarly about my own call to vocational ministry. I'd do it again to get where I am, but I would not recommend it as a model for others.

I grew up going to church. As a child, my parents, grandparents, and two great-aunts made sure I went—and they helped me love it. I made a profession of faith at age 13, and even though I was known as the risk-taker in the youth group, I was involved in all phases of church until I was 17.

Then I suffered some teenage setbacks, including a move to another state two weeks before the first day of class for my senior year in high school. Because of these emotional trials, I did what many young males did in 1970: I rebelled—hard. I started drinking and, when I went off to college the next year, I became involved on the fringes of the drug culture of that era.

A number of times I tried—and failed—to pull myself out of the downward spiral. I caught a glimpse of a Billy Graham crusade on TV and threw away some alcohol. The next week that recommitment faded. I decided to quit my habits the week before attending a Rolling Stones concert. Someone offered me something to take that night, and I remembered almost nothing of the music I heard.

A few weeks later I was in a particularly altered state of mind and asked some friends, "Where are we?" I had no idea where we were, even though the surroundings were clearly familiar to me. My friends laughed until they cried at my condition.

In that moment I hit rock bottom. In that moment, like the prodigal son, I came to myself. I remember feeling disgusted—and very helpless. I prayed, "Dear God, if you will get me home alive, I promise that tomorrow I am yours."

The next morning, I awoke at a friend's house. My head was turned toward a window, and I saw the sun. Remembering my promise, I gave thanks to God to be alive and safe. "I'm yours," I said.

I did not sense a call to ministry the morning after Christ rescued me from myself, but the transformation of that night started a year-long process of trying to understand what had happened and the implications of making a commitment to give myself totally to Christ.

The summer these events took place I worked as a manual laborer. On rainy days when we did not work, I went by my home church to visit with the new youth minister, Bob Crutcher. Bob helped me articulate my experience and, at the end of the summer, asked me to give my testimony to a group of college students. It was the first time I acknowledged my past and the change Christ had worked.

During my sophomore year in college Bob stayed in touch and nurtured my maturing faith. In March he asked me to serve as a youth intern in his ministry during the next summer. I resisted, saying, "You know the way I was just last summer. No one wants me working with their youth. I am not good enough to work in a church."

Bob told me, "People who feel worthy often don't work out. God only asks that you be willing."

That summer was a great experience. Naïve in some areas and overconfident in others, I made many mistakes. Bob cleaned up after me, kept offering encouragement, and gave me additional responsibilities.

Late in the summer our church experienced two tragic deaths in one week. The next Sunday our pastor changed his sermon topic to "The Immediacy of Time and Life." He preached about the fleeting nature of life, its unpredictability, and the need to address its weightier matters immediately. Late in the message he made the statement, "Too many people ask, 'Why should I serve Christ?' when they should be asking, 'Why *shouldn't* I serve Christ?'" I don't know if he was talking to me, but Christ was.

At lunch I told Bob that I felt called to ministry. He just looked at me and said, "I know. I hoped you would figure it out." That night I responded to the call during the invitation. I felt totally unworthy, but I was willing.

When I returned to college for the fall, I went to see a local pastor I had met before. He told me, "If you can do anything else in this life and be happy, do it. If not, you're called." At the time his words struck me as cynical. Over time their wisdom became apparent.

In my 20s and early 30s when ministry was hard and people proved difficult, I considered working in another field. That pastor's advice came back to mind. When I considered what else

I could do and be happy, the same answer came back to me time after time: nothing. I knew I was called.

The advice of Bob Crutcher and that pastor in my college town were the two best pieces of guidance I received as I sorted out exactly what Christ wanted me to do. Bob's words about worthiness and willingness shaped my understanding of grace that extended beyond salvation to ministry. The pastor's simple evaluation tool kept me going in doubtful times.

After the summer of my call, two more years of prayer and counseling with trusted mentors passed before I understood that the shape of my call included preaching. As college ended, I made plans to attend seminary and prepare to be a pastor.

Based on my own experience, I offer four pieces of advice for anyone trying to decide whether or not Christ is calling them to full-time Christian service.

First, there are no "worthy" people. If we take our theology seriously, the pool of God's potential candidates is filled with sinners. There is no one else; your willingness is what matters.

Second, the ministry has many unexpected demands. People will disappoint you. If there is anything else in this life you can do and find fulfillment, then do it. The statement is not cynical; rather, it speaks to the level of commitment it takes to stay with the call. If there are other paths that you think would be a better fit for your life, follow them. If not, you are called.

Third, find trusted mentors. Consider asking your church to hire a ministry coach for you. We all need a safe place to debrief and hear trusted advice to follow. I don't know what I would have done without the patience and wise counsel of experienced ministers.

Finally, do not expect to understand your call immediately. If God calls you at a young age, it will be impossible for you to imagine the variety of ways God might lead five or 10 years from now. Trust God for each day and the journey will begin to take shape before you.

Now I must answer the question I posed for the prodigal son: "Would I choose the same path again?" I would not choose to relive the despair or the helplessness of hitting rock bottom. My rebellious ways are not a model to follow in order to find Christ or discern a call. The risks are serious. But in the depths of those months during my 20th summer, Christ called my name and I came to myself. I wouldn't choose the same path, but knowing how God used those events I would endure them again for the sake of the high calling in Jesus Christ.

Joel Snider retired in 2016 from a 21-year pastorate at First Baptist Church of Rome, Ga. He became executive director of the Community Foundation for Greater Rome in 2018, and also continues to serve churches as a consultant and interim pastor. He and his wife, Cherry, continue to live in Rome.

I Love Serving as a Pastor

Dave Snyder

St. Louis, Missouri! That is where I was born and raised. My parents were, and still are, passionate about following Jesus. As a child, I was raised in a home with a clear and nurturing understanding of the gospel. I made my commitment to become a Jesus follower early in life, between the third and fourth grade. I understood sin and the need for a rescue.

Although I made my commitment to Christ at a young age, my journey of discipleship really took off in high school when I developed a deeper understanding of the gospel while dealing with adolescent struggles of sin and temptation. My love has grown since then, as I have realized the importance of daily time with my Savior. There have been bumps along the way, but his grace has been just as sufficient today as it was many years ago.

In high school my heart was set on music ministry. As a piano player, I hoped to enter the world of contemporary Christian music. Following this dream, I attended Murray State University in Murray, Ky., with a concentration in music education. This journey began with great excitement, until my heart and passion veered in a different direction.

In my second year of college, when I was 19 years old, the Lord graciously called me into serving his church in the role of a student pastor. I was told of a wonderful church down the road from the college in need of help with student ministry. West Fork Baptist Church in Murray, by God's design, gave me my first opportunity in fulfilling God's call.

I enjoyed every aspect of the church, particularly my work with students. West Fork provided opportunities for me to preach, lead, counsel, serve, and even sing! For eight months of my two-year tenure there was no pastor: I was given the pulpit. I imagine terrible sermons were delivered in this season, but God was faithful. Following my second year of serving this wonderful faith family, the Lord called me to First Baptist Murray. For my last year of college, I had the privilege of serving under the leadership of Boyd Smith, the veteran and well-loved student pastor. At FBC Murray I learned the dynamics of serving on a church staff and of working with a large church (FBC Murray had more than 500 weekly attenders).

After graduating from college, I followed the Lord's call to attend seminary at New Orleans Baptist Theological Seminary in Louisiana. Employment at a nearby hotel, in addition to summer camp ministry with FUGE camps, helped pay my bills. It was in New Orleans where I met my beloved Brooke. When my second year of seminary began, Hurricane Katrina arrived. The seminary campus was impacted and shut down, causing my future wife and me to move to Atlanta. God, in his perfect call, had Summit Baptist Church in Acworth, Ga., in store for us in the midst of this unexpected transition. Brooke was blessed to finish her PhD at Emory University in Atlanta, which was a major gift of God's provision as it is nearly impossible to transfer to another school during such rigorous studies.

For five years my time at Summit Baptist was deeply meaningful. The Lord provided more opportunities of pastoral ministry while leading the student ministry. In addition to my weekly expectations, I was blessed with pulpit time, hospital visits, weddings, counseling, and other pastoral ministry jobs. I learned lessons on deep trust and dependency on the Lord as the church experienced highs and lows. With low giving and budget cuts, I made the decision to look for new employment. This decision, by the providence of God, led us to CrossPoint church in Trussville, Ala.

I still remember walking into Pastor Ryan Whitley's office in my first month. My heart was set to grow as a student minister. With only a little more than six years of experience under my belt, I was convinced student ministry was my road for life—until retirement, at least. In my second to third year of student work, my heart began to see a bigger picture for God's call. Each pastoral opportunity given to me just fueled my soul for more. Every sermon, hospital visit, staff meeting, fellowship, deacon meeting, retreat, and other experiences piqued my curiosity about a senior pastor position. Of course, I was so busy with student work, I didn't pursue any of those thoughts, but they were there like hidden dreams.

In the summer of 2013 our second child was born, and I was accepted into the doctoral program at Southeastern Baptist Theological Seminary in Wake Forest, N.C. With a concentration on church leadership, I sought to grow as a potential senior pastor. Every long drive from Birmingham, Ala., to Wake Forest afforded me the time to pray and think on the future. As my studies in leadership grew, so did my desire for pastoring. Several phone calls home at night provided times for me to share my excitement with Brooke. God used my DMin journey to open my heart for his call into the senior pastorate. The steps ahead were graduation and finding the church he set. Graduation came as expected, but finding a church was difficult.

For two years it seemed that one door after another closed for me. Search committees could not get over my young age and lack of pastoral experience. Committees didn't recognize the 16 years of student ministry work in churches as enough evidence of readiness for the pastorate. Many nights of frustration and disappointment welcomed me like an unwanted guest. I was discouraged and often downtrodden. But God, in his gracious call, had First Baptist in Pensacola, Fla., ready for me. After a curious application sent to a search firm, the Lord led a wonderful process. The search team was gracious, excited, and genuine in the entire journey. What began as an early email of interest led to a divine call to the senior pastorate.

My role as an associate pastor in student ministry provided the right experience that God used to sharpen and refine his calling in my life. I learned under wonderful pastors and church staff. I received mentoring from both clergy and lay leaders. I cannot imagine the journey of God's call without the associate pastor chapter in the book. I'm so glad God is the author and I'm the trusted reader.

I love every aspect of the church. I love seeing multiple generations gather in praise and honor of the risen Savior. I love seeing lives changed by the power of the gospel. I love seeing laughter and tears shared with the family of faith. I love the privilege of preaching and hearing truth resonate the halls. I love singing songs from centuries ago or from this year.

The church is indeed the bride of Christ—and she is absolutely beautiful.

Dave Snyder serves as the senior pastor of First Baptist Church of Pensacola, Fla. He has a passion to preach, lead, and equip believers to fulfill the Great Commission. Dave and his wife, Brooke, have three children. He enjoys reading, journaling, visiting with people over coffee, and following St. Louis Cardinals baseball.

In the Right Place

Jim Somerville

When people find out that I grew up Presbyterian, they often want to know how I became Baptist. "Well," I say, "the short answer is that I fell in love with a pretty Baptist girl." And that usually satisfies them, but that's not the whole story.

I did fall in love with a pretty Baptist girl, and I ended up transferring from my college—St. Andrews Presbyterian in North Carolina—to hers—Georgetown College in Kentucky: a Baptist school. I had been there about two weeks when we had our first big fight, and it was a doozy. I came back to my dormitory room, sat on the edge of my bunk, and said, "Jim Somerville, this is the stupidest thing you have ever done: transferred to another school—for a girl!" But she did two things for which I will always be grateful: she got me to Georgetown, and she brought me to Faith Baptist Church.

That church met in a building that some people said looked like a gas station: an attempt at modern architecture on a severely limited budget. Cheap carpeting covered the concrete floor, the pulpit was made of plywood, and instead of pews there were folding chairs. But somehow it reminded me of the simple churches I had attended in my childhood, and when the pastor came out wearing a robe (just like a Presbyterian!) I was sold. His name was Bill Treadwell, and he preached a sermon that I was still thinking about the next day.

That's how it was with Bill. I wouldn't say he was the best preacher I ever heard but certainly one of the most thoughtful. He was a big man, with a big heart. He had an easy laugh and a way of pulling people into the life of that church so that it didn't take long for me to fall in love with Faith Baptist and fall in love with him. It would be another year before I learned that he had a daughter named Christy. She started as a freshman at Georgetown as I was entering my senior year. We went out a few times that fall, but then I pulled back. I didn't want things to get too serious; I had other plans. And yet, we ended up being good friends, and maybe more than friends.

After I graduated from college I went off to Boston, Massachusetts, to seek my fortune. I looked for it in radio, in television, in newspapers and magazines. But I didn't find it there. I kept thinking about that girl I had left behind. One day I quit my newspaper job, got in my car, and drove as far as Charleston, W.Va., before spending the night with friends. The next day I got up and drove the rest of the way to Georgetown.

I called Christy, pretending that I was still in Boston. I asked her if she wanted to go out for a pizza that night. She said she did. I told her I would be there in 30 minutes. She said, "Make it 45:

134

I'd like to take a shower first." She thought I was joking, but something inside her said, "Maybe not." She took that shower and when I rang the doorbell, there she was: in a terrycloth robe with a towel wrapped around her head. We went to Pizza Hut, and over a large pepperoni I asked her if she thought we could be more than friends. She said she was willing to try.

When her dad found out about it, he said if I was going to be hanging around, I might as well join the church. I said, "Well, I don't know . . . What do Baptists believe?" He told me Baptists believe in freedom: individual freedom, Bible freedom, church freedom, and religious freedom, explaining each one in detail. It all sounded good to me. But then he asked me what I believed.

As a lifelong Presbyterian, I told him: "I believe in God the Father Almighty, Maker of heaven and earth: And in Jesus Christ his only Son our Lord . . ." I rattled off the entire Apostle's Creed, right down to the part about "the resurrection of the body and the life ever-lasting." He was stunned. He said, "Do you really believe all that?" I thought about it for a second and then said, "I do." And then he said, "I think you'll make a good Baptist!" So, I joined the church the next Sunday. It wasn't long afterward that he asked if I would be inter-ested in serving as the part-time youth minister.

That wasn't a difficult decision. I liked kids and I had some free time, so I said yes. The next Wednesday night I found myself standing in front of the youth group trying to figure out what a part-time youth minister is supposed to do. It wasn't easy, but I learned as I went. I had a list with the names of all those kids in alphabetical order. It didn't take long to memorize it, and when I went running in the morning I would pray for each of them by name. When I got to work, I would sometimes catch myself looking out the window and thinking about what I could do with the group the next Wednesday night. I loved being a youth minister, and sometimes wished that I were independently wealthy so I could do it all the time. I didn't know, in those days, that some ministers actually got paid enough to live on.

In my role as a part-time staff member, I sometimes got to help out in worship on Sunday mornings. I would read Scripture, make announcements, or pray the pastoral prayer. Church members began to tell me I was good at those things, and then one night, when Christy and her mother were away, her father took me out for a steak dinner and asked me if I had ever thought about being a pastor.

Well, no! I never had. And I told him so. I could still remember the time someone had asked me, as a boy, if I were going to be a preacher like my daddy when I grew up and I had said, "No! No, no, NO! Absolutely not!" That answer was still inside me when Bill asked. I told him I was hoping to be rich and famous someday and I didn't think ministry was the way to do that. But he said, "I don't know. I've never been rich, but I've always had enough. And in the places I've served, people have always known who I was." I told him that's not what I meant and he said, "Okay, but at least promise me you'll think about it."

So, I did. And then I found that I couldn't stop thinking about it. I was hoping that God would make it clear to me, that sometime during the night I would hear a blast on a trumpet and the ceiling would open up and a scroll would roll down that read, "Jim Somerville, you are (or are not) being called into the ministry!" But it didn't happen like that.

A few weeks after that steak dinner, Bill invited me to go with him to visit the Baptist seminary in Louisville. I went and while I was there I asked every student who would talk to me, "How did you know that you were supposed to be a minister?" They didn't have very good answers. One said that he didn't know what else to do after college, so he came to seminary. Another said that his grandmother had always thought he would be a good preacher. That didn't seem like enough of a reason.

So, I went to see Paul Duke, the pastor of Highland Baptist Church in Louisville and someone I respected. I sat in his office for an hour explaining my dilemma, and when I finished he said, "It sounds like you've already made up your mind." I said, "What?" He said, "For the last 15 minutes instead of saying, '*If* I come to seminary,' you've been saying, '*When* I come to seminary.' It sounds to me like you've already made up your mind." I was amazed. I asked, "How did you do that?" Paul smiled and said, "I learned it in seminary—'Listen to the man!'"

It wasn't that Sunday or even the one after that, but it wasn't too much longer before the knowledge that was in my soul moved me to get up out of my pew and stumble down the aisle of Faith Baptist Church to tell Bill Treadwell I was ready to surrender to the call to ministry. I was like one of those first disciples, who wasn't even sure why he had let go of the nets, and who really wished he had something to hold on to. But it was too late. I had made a public decision. I had to follow through.

I had been at seminary only about two weeks when I had this wonderful sense of confirmation. I remember when it happened. I was on my way to class and when I opened the door and stepped into Norton Hall I thought, "I'm in the right place." What a relief!

I had come to seminary thinking I would major in media ministry and that one day it would be my job to make Christian television shows. But then I got a request from a pastor search committee in a little town not far away, asking if I would be willing to come for an interview. To my surprise, I said yes, and the next thing I knew I was preaching a trial sermon at New Castle Baptist Church.

After my sermon, the members called me to be their pastor. Did they know how little I knew? They might have, because Rex Prather, the chair of the pastor search committee, told the church, "We know Jim has never done this before. He has no idea what he's doing. But we're going to let him practice on us." Those were the kindest words he could have said, and probably the smartest, because then, every time I messed up, someone would say, "Still practicing, huh?" But a few weeks into that job I presided over communion for the first time, and as I stood behind that table holding the broken bread that represented the broken body of Christ, I knew what I knew, and what I knew was this:

I had found my calling.

Jim Somerville is the senior minister at First Baptist Church in Richmond, Va. He previously served as the pastor of the First Baptist Church of the City of Washington, D.C., and Wingate Baptist Church in Wingate, N.C. In his spare time Jim enjoys traveling, backpacking, sailing, reading, watching movies, and spending time with his family. He and his wife, Christy, have two daughters, Ellie and Catherine.

A Call to Love

Chris Thomas

Growing up in the Deep South, you tend to have someone in your family who is a preacher, whether it is an uncle, grandfather, cousin, etc. Of course, if you did not have a preacher in the family, you were at least part of a good, church-going family. That is, unless you were me.

See, my folks didn't go to church, at least not after the 1980s. We went when I was small child, but after my parents' divorce, the death of my grandfather, and the often-unfiltered language and grittiness of my grandmother, our absence may have been a welcomed one to some of those (as Flannery O'Connor may have called them) good, country people.

I had little to no exposure to church after those days, until I met my best friend John in the third grade. John and his family had just moved from Mobile, where his dad had been a pastor and adjunct professor of religion. John and I became instant friends, mostly because we were the two new kids in the class. He would invite me to VBS, RA campouts, and the weekly Wednesday night church gatherings, where we mostly played touch football in the church yard. I would occasionally spend Saturday night at his house and go with him to church in the morning to hear his dad preach.

(Before I go any further, I must tell you how important John and his father—also named John—became in my life, to my faith, and to my calling. Without John's friendship, I would have likely never set foot inside a church outside of a funeral or wedding or known what it was like to be a *real* Christian. Without his dad's presence in my life [in many ways, as if he were my own father], I would have never gone to college, never met my wife, never learned that this calling can be one that truly changes another's life forever. I owe them more than I can ever repay. I think there's a word for that: grace.)

Because of my friendship with John, there were two degrees of separation between the church and me. It was like my life and Christ's calling were two parallel highways that would come close to each other only to widen the gap a little farther down the way, but always moving toward some inevitable merger into one road, one way. Those two roads shared some pavement my senior year of high school when I joined the church softball team of Goodman Baptist Church, the church where John was a member and where his dad had been called to be pastor some years before (he was director of missions for the county Baptist association by that time). The church softball team was a way to do something I had always loved: play baseball, sort of.

I worked three jobs in high school, so extracurricular sports were not an option for me, with their enormous time commitments and usually high costs for equipment. Church softball, however, was pretty cheap, and the only time commitment was one Sunday service per month. I signed up to play and figured if I could make it one Sunday a month, I could probably do every Sunday . . . which turned into every Wednesday evening prayer meeting . . . which turned into every Sunday night discipleship training class and worship service.

I was going to church all the time. Why? Because I had found this strange thing happening. These people, with whom I initially just wanted to play softball, were treating me like I was more than some poor kid with good grades. These people acted like they actually missed me when I wasn't around, like they actually cared about me, as if their joy and sorrow were caught up in my own. It felt to me like what I imagined those families in cable television Christmas movies were like. There's a word for that: love. These people actually loved me, and the only reason I could figure they loved me had something to do with this Jesus they were always singing about, praying to, and telling other folks about. Jesus . . . that's what it was.

My need for Jesus and his people became glaringly clear after I graduated from high school. I had graduated as valedictorian, with a scholarship to a technical school and a job as a fleet mechanic for the school district. This was as good as my life could hope to get. No one in my family had gone on to any kind of school after high school, and the job I had waiting was going to be a "gravy train with biscuit wheels" in the world of auto and diesel repair. All I had to do was walk across the stage, get my diploma, and life would unroll before me. I nailed the graduation, but when I returned to work two days later I was told I had "worked myself out of a job," and they wouldn't be keeping me on as a fleet mechanic. It was the worst news of my life. Things fell apart in a day. That was May of 2002.

I found a new job, never went to the technical school, and moved in with my dad, who happened to live closer to my church. This community of faith became my refuge, the place and people in whom I could find some steadiness, some sense that the wheels hadn't come completely off yet. I wanted to be a part of this community, so I was baptized in September of 2002. I distinctly remember thinking to myself, "Boy, you have gone and done it now. They all saw what you did, and you can't take it back." It was the hinge around which my entire life turned; I mean that as much as anyone can mean anything.

After my baptism I poured over the King James Bible the church had given me. I wanted to know more about Jesus, more about what his words meant, more about the purpose of my life, more about everything. I would have conversations with our pastor, with John's dad, with my Sunday School teachers (who would mostly tell me to ask the pastor). I was restless. It seemed to me that the only thing that mattered, the only thing any of us is called to do, was to follow Jesus, to do what Jesus did, to live as Jesus lived. I couldn't shake this feeling that I wasn't doing everything I could with everything Christ had given me. Then I went to Mobile, Ala.

Every summer our local Baptist association took a mission trip to southwest Alabama, and in the summer of 2003 I went. I wanted to spend time with people I came to love—friends and folks who were closer than family. I went to do what Jesus called us all to do: love others.

John and I drove down a couple of days after everyone else because we had class (I had enrolled in the local community college in hopes of getting some traction and direction for my life). When we arrived at the park where we were conducting a Backyard Bible Club, there was a large group of kids gathered around our friends who were already there, playing some version of "duck, duck, goose." As we were walking over to them, I noticed one child, about four or five years old, sitting by himself on the benches on the other side of the park. I was told he was being disruptive and uncooperative, causing trouble with the rest of the kids.

I decided there were enough volunteers helping with that gaggle of kids, so I went over to the kid sitting on the bench. His name was Josh, but I called him "Wild Man." I asked him if he liked Spider-Man (he was wearing a Spider-Man t-shirt): no response. I asked if he wanted to go play with the other kids: no response. I asked if he wanted a piggy-back ride: his face lit up as if I had offered him a rocket ride to the moon. "Wild Man" and I were inseparable the rest of the week.

There was a distinct moment in our time together when I knew what God was calling me to do. It was the last day of our time there. Wild Man and I were sitting on a bench, watching a couple of the volunteers do a flannelgraph presentation of Jesus' last supper with his disciples, when Wild Man leaned his head on my arm as I put my cap on his head. I told him that Jesus loved him and that I loved him. He looked up at me and said, "I love you too." It broke me. I saw in that little boy's eyes someone who just needed to be told he was loved, someone who just needed to hear that love wasn't based on who you are or what you've done, someone who just wanted to be loved even if he had misbehaved more than once. I saw in that little boy's eyes Christ calling me to tell people—to show people—love, God's love.

After the story was over, all of the kids went inside the building at the park for cookies and Capri Suns. As they were all running toward the building, my pastor Jerry (another man to whom I owe a great deal) came and put his hand on my shoulder and said, "You know what God is calling you to, don't you?" I couldn't even say the word, but I thought it: "Yes." As it turns out, Jerry and a few other men in our church were meeting together before Sunday School every week to pray for me, because Jerry sensed that God might be calling me to ministry. When I announced it to our church, more than a few people said to me, "I knew it!"

Since that day I have pursued this calling. I wanted to learn, so I transferred from the community college to Samford University to study religion. After graduating from Samford, I attended Truett Seminary at Baylor University on a full scholarship, and I'm currently pursuing a doctorate at McAfee School of Theology of Mercer University. I've served as the pastor of churches in Texas and Alabama, and traveled all over the world to lead camps, install water pumps, build schools, feed children, play games, and preach, teach, and show this love of Christ that has forever changed me.

Even when it's rough, when business meetings are frustrating, when someone doesn't like what I said in a sermon, when committee meetings are long, tedious, and pointless, when budgets are tight and folks are using their money as a mechanism for power, when all the things that pastors gripe about when they gather together are pressing in on me, I still thank God for this calling. You see, my calling isn't a professional decision: it's a life transformation. My calling isn't just about how I'll earn a living; it's my very life.

To me, the call from Christ is to "come and follow," and that means with all that I am, all that I have, all that I do. For me, that calling was one that could not simply be a piece of my life; it had to be the whole thing. I pray he keeps calling me—even when I want to quit, even when I don't think I deserve to be called, even when I daydream about managing an AutoZone—because I know there are so many out there like "Wild Man" who just need someone to tell them, to show them, they are loved, just as they are. And, Christ compels me to be one who tells them, one who shows them, with all that I am. I think there's a word for that: calling.

Chris Thomas is the pastor of First Baptist Church of Williams near Jacksonville, Ala. In addition to his pastoral responsibilities he enjoys working with his hands, learning new skills, and spending time with his wife, Sallie, and their energetic sons, Kohl and Carter.

Connected Calling

Garrett Vickrey

"You're too young." I heard this frequently my first year as a pastor. I also heard, "You're too liberal. It's not your fault; it's that East Coast seminary."

A group of malcontents within the church paraded into my office over the course of a month and, one by one, told me I should consider moving on. A few even offered me the role of young adult minister, if I chose to stay. I declined. They encouraged me to consider another calling. They said, "You're a sharp kid. You can do a lot of things. This church will take care of you and your family. But, you're too young for this responsibility. You don't have the experience. You don't have the know-how to *fix* this place."

I stayed. About half of this small group of dissidents left. And once the toxin of their discontent passed through our system, the church was able to focus again on what we do best—mission. I have a growing suspicion that even "experienced" pastors do not have the power to *fix* a church. That power resides in the healing hands of Christ's body.

Perhaps the saddest part of this church crisis was that this group of malcontent congregants was led by malcontent former ministers. These were people who had responded to the call of God upon their lives and given their lives in service to the church. Most of these former ministers within this group spent the majority of their careers in associate pastor roles at various churches. The look of jealousy in their eyes was hard to miss as they leered at a 30-year-old taking on a role they once coveted.

Six years later, I think back on that first year with gratitude for all the people who carried me through a difficult time. Sure, I had a lot to lose. But I came to slowly understand how much others had invested in me. The search committee prayed and searched for a new minister for 18 months following the retirement of their longtime beloved pastor. Mentors and colleagues spent hours on the phone with me going over how to communicate and manage this conflict within the church. My parents, siblings, friends, and spouse supported me and helped me to understand and respond to my sense of calling. This calling was not mine alone. In fact, the connection of my calling gave me confidence to do the work when the "results" and environment in which I was ministering were unfavorable.

I am the son of a pastor. My father, Ray Vickrey, was the pastor of Royal Lane Baptist Church in Dallas, Texas, for 26 years. He retired from Royal Lane the same year I started full-time ministry on staff at Myers Park Baptist Church in Charlotte, N.C. Royal Lane was my home—more so than the house I lived in growing up. After all, I was probably at the church more than my house anyway.

As a teenager, I remember thinking that being a pastor would be a terrible job. Writing a sermon every week was like being doomed to homework every weekend for the rest of your life. Surely, there must be better jobs. But I was in church all the time. Church people taught me what to celebrate. They taught me the injustices worthy of anger. They taught me about friendship and community. These people helped me to better understand who I am. They were my home, and everyone needs a home.

In college I struggled with discerning a call to ministry. I had opportunities to teach youth Sunday School. I served on mission teams rebuilding houses. I wondered if the deep-seated desire within me to create communities of faith like what I had known at Royal Lane was what a call to ministry "sounded" like. I also wondered if I was just wandering into the family business. Am I following God's call or following in the footsteps of my father? I came to realize that maybe it was a little of both. And that maybe that was okay. Even now, I feel as if my father's call and mine are intrinsically connected.

The summer after I graduated from college I worked as a student intern at Wilshire Baptist Church in Dallas. I had been accepted to Wake Forest University School of Divinity for the fall. I worked alongside Darren Dement that summer and learned the youth ministry trade from a true professional. Wilshire also had a cadre of young ministers in its residency program. Seeing them in action made ministry seem doable. The way the church trusted them and learned from them made it seem like there might be other churches out there that would not write off someone for being "too young."

And yet, I still was not sure I wanted to pursue this calling. If I left home (if I left Texas), would I ever come back? My parents were getting older. My dad was 71. Would he be around much longer? Jesus' advice in the New Testament (Luke 9:59-60) left me uncomforted.

So, I delayed divinity school and got a job. I waited tables at a terrible Mexican food restaurant. It closed the next year. I made enough money that fall to buy *a* book in divinity school. While the monetary compensation was lacking in the service industry, the bounty of sermon illustrations from my time in the restaurant business was generous.

January came. My father and I packed up my car and headed down the long road from Dallas to Winston-Salem, N.C. We traveled Interstate 20. What I didn't know at the time was how well acquainted my father was with this highway.

My dad grew up in Galena Park, a ship channel suburb of Houston. I have never met anyone else from Galena Park. Most people from Houston have no idea where it is. It is poor and overlooked. It is the kind of town Bruce Springsteen sings about making it out of.

My dad discerned a call to ministry at an early age. He was a good athlete who earned a track scholarship to Baylor University. At Baylor he ran the 440 and did the long jump. In the days before track and field in the U.S. adopted the metric system, the 440 was the precursor to the 400 meters. Baylor always excelled in this event. My dad was the Southwest Conference champion for two consecutive years in the long jump, and in 1956 he was a member of the

440-yard relay team that equaled the world record at that time. Once he graduated, he headed to Southwestern Baptist Theological Seminary in Fort Worth.

In Texas Baptist life we have a formula: athlete + preacher = golden boy. Ray Vickrey was set up well for a "successful ministry." He was married with two kids and ready to start his life in ministry somewhere. Then it all fell apart.

His marriage ended in divorce when he was 30 years old. For a Baptist minister of the time, this also meant the end of his career. The calling he had followed from his youth appeared to come to a swift and crushing end.

A few years later his ex-wife and his two children moved across the country from Fort Worth to Columbia, S.C., where her new husband had a new job. He, too, was a pastor who had to find a new calling with his "modern" family. And so, for the next decade my dad and his new wife (I call her Mom) traveled from Texas to South Carolina on Interstate 20. The interstate built to connect became a symbol of separation. That highway represented loss of family and loss of vocation. As they drove the 16 hours each way to pick up the kids, my parents would talk about the kind of church that would one day call them. Most days, this pastoral dream seemed as far away as the kids they loved.

Sometimes dreams come true. In 1981 my dad was called as the pastor of Royal Lane Baptist Church. I was three months old at the time. Finally, after two decades, he found a church willing to take a risk on a "divorced pastor." This second shot at the pastoral life was a long time coming. The dream deferred decades earlier finally came true. My dad had applied to churches for years, only to be rejected. Feeling like his divorce was a scarlet letter, he must have wondered if this day would ever come. Royal Lane lived grace, mercy, and compassion. And, that congregation was thrilled to call a pastor who knew mercy and grace are hard-won in this world. After years of driving up and down I-20 wondering if ministry was still a possibility, at 48 years old my dad accepted his first full-time call.

I wonder what was going through his mind along the way to Wake Forest. On that road where he had dropped off his kids summer after summer decades before, he was once again leaving a child on the other side of the country. How many times would he go through this? (I cried when I left my child at kindergarten—and that's just down the street from my house.)

This calling is one we share. As I was learning new things and expanding my knowledge in divinity school, my father's memory waned. He had trouble completing sentences. He had trouble remembering names. His preaching suffered, and he no longer felt like he could do the work in a way that was acceptable to him. He was 74 and the road ahead was becoming clearer: dementia, Alzheimer's, deterioration of the mind within a healthy body. He would never be the same.

After a few years of youth ministry I was feeling a bit burned out by retreats, camps, and mission trips. I wanted to minister to people of diverse generations, and since I had seen people from the pastoral residency at Wilshire get actual jobs as pastors at a young age, I thought I should do that. So, I moved back to Dallas, three years into that journey we call "Dad's memory problems." This time we returned home by a different road. Instead of going down I-20, we took I-40 across Tennessee. And my wife and I brought our three-month-old baby with us.

Now, when I hear that I am too young to be a pastor I laugh. Maybe they are right. I would be a better minister were I ministering with the scars of lost relationships, lost dreams, and lost vocational aspirations. I would know more about the grace and mercy Jesus talked about.

Remembering those phony rebukes from my first year, I recognize the privilege I possess. To be called to minister in the churches I have is a great privilege. In a way, I get to do what my father did not get to do. Maybe there's a kind of redemption there for him. He can't give voice to that now, but every now and then I think I can see it in his eyes.

Garrett Vickrey is the senior pastor of Woodland Baptist Church in San Antonio, Texas. A graduate of Baylor University and Wake Forest University School of Divinity, he previously served on the staff of Wilshire Baptist Church in Dallas, Texas, and Myers Park Baptist Church in Charlotte, N.C. Garrett and his wife, Cameron, have three daughters, Finley, Zetta, and Sloane.

A Convincing Call,
A Compelling Mission

Bill Wilson

~

I had a stock answer for the question, "What do you want to be when you grow up?" To everyone who asked, I responded: a professional ball player, and then president of the United States.

Growing up as a firstborn pastor's son, many people had assumed that ministry would be my preferred vocational option. Our ministry household was a pleasant one, and the two churches my father served as pastor were thriving and successful. He and my family provided me a positive and encouraging role model, and the churches were happy, growing and nurturing.

However, I was not of the opinion that I was destined for ministry. Instead, I vacillated between which professional sport I would play: baseball, basketball, or football. Perhaps I'd be the first to play all three as a successful professional! My delusions of grandeur knew no bounds. It wasn't long before my limited physical skills on the field or court became apparent, and I had to consider other options.

Genuinely wrestling with college and career choices had just begun for me in those middle adolescent years. I loved politics, was elected president of my high school, and began to think that a law degree, vast wealth, and political stardom were in my future. Gradually, I found an alternative calling taking root deep within me as our church began to emphasize the need to focus our attention outward and not just inward.

Our youth group, under the relentless pressure of wise leaders, was challenged to consider the idea that a self-serving life was not the way of Jesus. As part of that strategy, we took the initiative to go on a mission trip to a rural Appalachian area where we would serve others rather than be served. Fifty years ago, such personal engagement was a new and innovative way of doing missions. Most of us simply gave money to enable others to engage in missions. We were actually going to get our privileged, soft, white hands dirty. Little did I know what awaited me.

I was lying on my back on a mountaintop in rural West Virginia when I first saw the Milky Way and simultaneously sensed God's overwhelming call to ministry. It was the summer prior to my final year in high school when our youth group ventured to that rural county to work with kids in desperate need. In that moment of sensing the vastness of the universe, I also sensed the depth of meaning that I had only found in such mission settings.

That week we spent time working with people in desperate need as we assisted a local faith-based nonprofit led by a passionate and motivated leader named Billy. I was mesmerized by his integration of a deep faith and sincere love for the people of that Appalachian community. The results were astounding. Everywhere we went we were welcomed and treated like special guests. People told us how much they loved Billy and how much they knew he loved them. Billy made a huge difference in the lives of those people because he gave himself to them out of a deep calling. I came to crave that depth of calling in my own life.

The trajectory of my life's journey changed that week. In the midst of the starkest poverty I had ever seen, alongside some of the most stunning beauty on the planet, my calling crystalized. Those missional ideas that had been planted deep within my soul began to grow and bear fruit. I found in that experience more fulfillment than any other success had ever brought me. I found a longed-for intersection between my gifts and the world's needs. From that day forward I have been living out my call to help others find the same depth of meaning.

The driving metaphor for my missional call has evolved into a simple personal mission statement: My mission in life is to help grow the influence of Jesus through groups, organizations, and people. Over the course of more than 40 years the location and circumstances of living out that call have changed, but the call remains consistent.

For a decade I was a youth minister, and my focus was on motivating and helping students grow into the person Christ intended them to be. For 25 years and in three churches I was a pastor, and my passion and calling took another approach to faith development. For the last decade I have found my calling to be in ministry to a more diverse community of churches and clergy across the country as a coach, mentor, and consultant.

In every context and venue, I filter opportunities and challenges through the lens of whether and how this will grow the impact and influence of Christ in the lives of those involved and those yet-to-be involved. Keeping that focus clear and crisp is an ongoing challenge, but one that keeps me motivated and oriented to my missional calling.

The power of a compelling mission in life is hard to overstate. For individuals, organizations, and churches, such a vision of where God is leading is an essential ingredient. Without it, we are subject to the whims of opinion, the winds of culture, and the unpredictability of circumstances. With it, we are able to hold fast to our own sense of call.

Across the years I have found myself in the midst of my share of disappointments and failures. Sometimes those were of my doing; other times my life was impacted by the failures of others. More than once I have wondered if my commitment to ministry would endure the ups and downs of life in the church! In every circumstance I have rediscovered the power of that missional vision to guide me through the challenges of the moment. Whether I am tempted to think too much or too little of myself and my career, I turn to that calling "to grow the influence of Jesus through groups, organizations, and people." That remains the constant in the midst of the change and chaos that often surrounds me. When I steadfastly say yes to that calling, I can say either no or yes to opportunities with conviction.

That coherence and alignment have helped lower my anxiety and tempered a strong need to please others. The mission is now central—not approval from others, financial gain, or social status. When I am able to truly put first things first, the resulting spiritual, physical, emotional, and mental health that Christ brings is profound.

I sense that many of us desperately need that clear sense of mission and purpose. We all are tempted to allow others to define us and dictate to us what success looks like in our life. Being laser-focused upon our calling enables us to say no to the imposters that lure us away from our reason for being.

It also engages our imagination when we realize that our calling is more substantial than our current setting. We are freed from the false thinking that our job is our identity. When calling transcends a job, then the Latin meaning of vocation (*vocare*=calling) begins to make sense to us. My vocation is my calling. My job is where I am living out my calling today. Jobs come and go, but my calling, my vocation, is ongoing. Keeping that distinction clear is essential for a healthy spiritual life.

In this final quarter of my vocational life I have sensed God's calling to transition away from working with one church and staff to working with multiple dozens of churches, clergy, and laity across the country. It was a hard call, to say the least. Leaving the comfort and security of a career and a remarkable church that was doing amazing things was gut-wrenching. Taking a significant pay cut and forfeiting 25 years of equity in a house meant a very different financial future for my family. As much as I wanted to ignore it, the call was clear and unrelenting. God had another setting for me to live out my calling. I finally decided I either had to say yes to the opportunity or stop preaching the necessity of our obedience to God's leadership. Saying yes to that call has opened up a new horizon in my life that I would have otherwise missed.

Much like that night on a mountaintop in West Virginia, God has overwhelmed me with the opportunities before the church in the 21st century. The scale of the looming challenges faced by congregations and ministers at times bewilders me. We really are in a season of dramatic change and realignment among the churches and faith communities of North America. Fear and anxiety rule, and the future can easily look bleak.

On other days I am reminded that God's people often do our best work when we forego our self-confidence and humbly place our lives, careers, and futures in God's hands. Our humility and awareness of the limits of our gifts and resources can lead us toward a new day of obedience. Being able to hold fast to a profound sense of call gives me confidence in the face of immense challenges.

While I expect the venues and vehicles for living out my calling to continue to change, what will not change is that deep calling "to grow the influence of Jesus through groups, organizations, and people." As I consistently pursue that calling, my prayer is that I will be continually transformed into more of the person God intends me to be. I am grateful beyond words that the call that began one night on a mountaintop has remained vibrant and compelling for me.

William "Bill" Wilson founded the Center for Healthy Churches in January of 2014, following service as president of the Center for Congregational Health at Wake Forest Baptist Health since 2009. Previously he served as the pastor of First Baptist Church of Dalton, Ga., for six years. He brings more than 33 years of local church ministry experience to CHC, having served as the pastor in two churches in Virginia (Farmville Baptist and First Baptist in Waynesboro) and on a church staff in South Carolina. Bill has led each of the churches he has served into a time of significant growth and expansion of ministry. He is the director of CHC.

Afterword:
Cultivating a Culture of Call

Bill Wilson

Nearly all observers of the 21ˢᵗ-century church in the United States agree that the next genera-tion of leadership is a cause for concern. Many write, blog, tweet, and generally lament the state of leadership cultivation and training, or lack thereof. Far too many congregations no longer encourage young people and laity to consider vocational ministry. Many congregations cannot remember the last time someone from their ranks sensed a call to vocational ministry and followed that call to licensing, ordination, or both.

Those who study such things know that a minority of our congregations produce a majority of our clergy. What is it about the culture of those churches that encourages a call to ministry among their members? How do they create a "culture of call" that invites parishioners to consider deeply the possibility that God may be leading them into vocational ministry?

Melissa Wiginton served for several years at the Fund for Theological Education before moving to Austin Presbyterian Theological Seminary. She, as well as anyone I know, has been a prophetic voice in this arena of "call." I once heard her describe the major traits of churches that are successful at creating this calling culture. She identified four characteristics of a "calling church":

1. **A place where something is at stake:** Calling churches do more than busywork; they engage many people in life-changing ministry. Their members are passionate about their church and its mission. They invest in youth and children's ministry that is more than fun and games.
2. **A church that is a seat of resistance:** Calling churches consistently sound a counter-cultural message about what matters most. They hold up a vision of being active in the Kingdom of God that stands in opposition to much of what 21ˢᵗ-century American culture says is important.
3. **A church that is a site of interpretation:** Calling churches regularly tell stories of how God is at work in the lives of their people. They read and tell the stories of the Bible. They name people's gifts and encourage them to use their gifts and their passion under the direction of the Holy Spirit.
4. **A church that provides a "good enough" home:** Calling churches recognize that perfection is not possible or necessary. They create a culture that challenges people internally (spiritual life) and externally (spiritual habits). They are committed to quality, but not perfectionism. They foster intergenerational relationship and regularly "apprenticize" their young people.

As I journey in and out of congregations, I am constantly looking and listening for these characteristics of a calling culture. All too often, congregations are so focused on survival that they have grown blind to the call to propagate and reproduce leaders. Many times our youth and children's ministries have been reduced to a consumer model focused on customer satisfaction rather than discipleship.

As the ministerial son of a minister and the father of a minister, I feel this tension in special ways. As an observer of churches in the U.S, I am burdened for the next generation of leadership and the question of where leaders will come from. I am increasingly convinced that healthy churches are like healthy plants: they produce leadership fruit. While that fruit is complex and multifaceted, at least part of what it must be about is a next generation of leaders who want to be involved in ministry as a vocation.

Thus, every congregation needs to ask itself the hard questions that accompany our efforts to reproduce leaders. What is your congregation doing and saying about this issue? To ignore it is to put your future in peril. To ignore it is to bypass a significant part of Jesus' three years of earthly ministry.

On the other hand, when we are engaged in significant ministry that is balanced between an internal and an external focus, when we challenge cultural norms rather than embrace them, when we live into our status as "exiles" (Tim Keller) or "resident aliens" (Stanley Hauerwas) in our culture, when we provide life-changing mission events and sound a relentless biblical call to life-stewardship, then I believe we will find our people responding in the affirmative to the leadership of the Holy Spirit.

I am thankful for the privilege of having seen several young people and adults enter vocational ministry from the churches I have served. In nearly every case they came out of a congregation that had made a deliberate effort to hold up ministry as a viable and fulfilling vocation. Many had been given the gift of mentors and encouragers who had called out their gifts and served as a "cloud of witnesses" for their journey.

Does that describe the culture of your congregation? If not, what would it look like to become more proactive as a calling congregation? Healthy churches need to ask and answer those questions.